GET
STARTED IN
WRITING
YOUNG
ADULT
FICTION

Teach®
Yourself

Get
Started in
Writing
Young
Adult
Fiction

Juliet Mushens

First published in Great Britain in 2015 by John Murray Learning. An Hachette UK company.

First published in US in 2015 by The McGraw-Hill Companies, Inc.

British Library Cataloguing in Publication Data: a catalogue record for this title is available from the British Library.

Library of Congress Catalog Card Number: on file.

Paperback ISBN 978 1 473 60707 1

Ebook ISBN 978 1 473 60708 8

3

Typeset by Cenveo® Publisher Services.

Printed and bound in Great Britain by CPI Group (UK) Ltd., Croydon, CRO 4YY.

John Murray Learning policy is to use papers that are natural, renewable and recyclable products and made from wood grown in sustainable forests. The logging and manufacturing processes are expected to conform to the environmental regulations of the country of origin.

John Murray Learning
Carmelite House
50 Victoria Embankment
London EC4Y 0DZ
www.hodder.co.uk

Also available in ebook

For Anne, Jeffrey and Lucy –
thanks for everything.

Acknowledgements

Thanks to the team at John Murray Learning: my original editor, Jamie Joseph, who commissioned this book, my publicist Lyndsey Ng, and my editors Jonathan Shipley and Robert Anderson.

Thanks again to my parents, Jeffrey and Anne, and my sister, Lucy, for support throughout – and for the loan of a computer and printer!

Thanks to Sarah Manning, and to my other colleagues at The Agency Group. Thanks to Molly Ker Hawn, Ed Wilson, Suzie Doore and Julia Churchill: publishing folk who are always full of helpful advice and insights.

The biggest thanks goes to all of my authors – Team Mushens – who make this job an absolute joy. I couldn't do it without you.

ACKNOWLEDGMENTS

Contents

About the author

Juliet Mushens works as a literary agent in the UK Literary Division of The Agency Group, representing a list of best-selling fiction and non-fiction writers. After reading history at Cambridge, she began her publishing career at HarperCollins in 2008 and became an agent in 2011. She was picked as a Bookseller Rising Star in 2012 and shortlisted for the Kim Scott Walwyn Prize for excellence in women in publishing in 2013 and for the Literary Agent of the Year award in 2014. You can find her on Twitter as @mushenska.

Introduction

Many people long to write a novel for young adults, but have no idea where to begin. How long should the book be? How do you come up with ideas? What makes a book suitable for a young-adult (YA) audience? How do you structure a narrative? How do you keep the reader intrigued by the story? What is my genre? How do I go about getting my work published? These are all valid questions but they can pose major stumbling blocks for a writer who has never written a book before. It is very easy to become fixated on these questions and to put off writing until you feel that you have all the answers. This book aims to help you answer those questions, and to realize that, even if you are not able to answer all of these questions right away, it should not stop you from beginning your young adult novel.

I am a literary agent in the UK and I have worked in publishing for six years, as a publisher as well as a literary agent. I have worked extensively with YA authors who are just starting out as well as with established and successful 'brand' authors. Supervising creative writing dissertations and judging literary prizes have also helped me identify the key issues faced by writers, and establish how to overcome these problems. I know better than most how daunting the process can be. Some of my most successful YA authors were once where you are now – wondering how to finish their novel, or even how to start it! I know from talking to them how daunting the publishing world can seem to an outsider, and how having someone who works in this world explain the process to you is invaluable. Not everyone has the chance to attend writing conferences, or pay for expensive writing courses, so this book aims to give you an equivalent experience and to help you on your way to successfully completing your YA novel.

Get Started in Writing Young Adult Fiction aims to offer support to people who are working on their first young adult novel and who are looking for guidance on how to begin, how to edit, and how to publish. It clears up many of the key queries about the process of writing your young adult novel and breaks the process down into bite-sized chunks which make getting started seem much more manageable. It offers sensible and easy-to-follow advice on everything from how to develop a plot and structure and writing believable characters and developing dialogue, right the way through to submitting the work to agents, self-publishing and more. Each chapter deals with one aspect of the writing process: offering advice, giving examples from my own experience, and giving several writing exercises for you to follow.

This guide is designed to be used as a 'teach yourself' tool and the experience will be equivalent to attending a creative writing course, lectures and writing groups. One of the key skills for the writer to learn is how to edit and, by doing the edit exercises and the workshop exercises, you will learn how to critique and improve your own work. You will get the most out of this book if you make sure you do every exercise as you go through the book: do not be afraid to repeat exercises, or to try them again. Writing is like many skills in that the more you do it, and the more seriously you take it, the better the results will be. Spending the time to think seriously about the exercises, edit and workshop parts of the book will help you develop the skills necessary to become a successful writer. If you go back to the beginning of the book once you have completed it and try the exercises again, you will be able to see the difference and improvement in your own writing. As Stephen King has said: 'When you write a book, you spend day after day scanning and identifying the trees. When you're done, you have to step back and look at the forest.'

The guide contains four different kinds of exercise: workshop, write, snapshot, and edit. The write exercise will be a practical one – a chance for you to have a go at setting down creative words on paper, based around the topic we have just looked at in a chapter. The snapshot will be a short exercise, often used to kickstart ideas or brainstorm, or to help you write a concise piece of work. The workshop and edit exercises are key, as they will help you learn to polish and revisit your work as we progress through the guide. They will also teach you to reflect on a piece of work, and to answer a series of guided questions, with the aim of helping you learn to be your own harshest critic. The guide also contains key ideas and focus points – simple yet important concepts for you to grasp when working on your book. The book is interspersed with quotes from writers and editors, which either elucidate some of the points discussed or act as inspirational and encouraging words. Even the most successful writer started somewhere, and many of them understand the stress of the process, as well as the joy. Their insights can really bring sticky points to life for the reader.

The book is designed to be used sequentially. The early chapters of the book focus on coming up with ideas, plotting, structuring, and establishing character and dialogue. The book will talk you through developing ideas, worldbuilding and plotting a novel, with related exercises throughout to expand on the points discussed and to help you apply them in a practical way. If you follow all of these workshop exercises, by the end of the book you should either have a completed novel, or have a large chunk of material which will set you well on your way to reaching the finish line.

The advice is straightforward and accessible, and is specifically designed to build your confidence – this confidence is key to setting that story down on paper! By the time you are three-quarters of the way through the book you will understand the skills, discipline and techniques necessary to write your novel.

In this book we will also look in depth at the different routes available to you once you have completed and polished your novel. Perhaps you just want something to keep for yourself and read to your children. But perhaps you are interested in finding a literary agent and attempting to become traditionally published. We will look in depth at hints and tips to achieve that. Self-publishing has made it a lot easier for anyone to get their work out there. However, when writing specifically for a young-adult market it is important to consider whether self-publishing is the best route to reach them. Certainly, some self-published writers have great success visiting schools and selling copies directly there. It is important to consider whether or not this route will be one you are able to take: perhaps the thought of speaking to a hall full of children fills you with dread! If you plan to digitally self-publish, we will look at best practice, resources and support, and how best to get your work noticed by teenagers online. The final chapters of the book will offer you an insight into how to secure a literary agent, how traditional publishing works, and whether self-publishing might be the best route for you to take.

As an established literary agent, I receive upwards of 600 submissions a month and approximately 50 per cent of these are aimed at a YA audience. I am skilled at spotting books that stand out from the crowd, as well as identifying the mistakes which most commonly slip through the net. In a competitive market you need to ensure that your book is as polished and punchy as possible and that it catches the eye of a literary agent and a publisher, as well as your eventual target market. Whether it is unbelievable dialogue, a voice that does not feel plausible for the audience you are writing for, or too much exposition, I draw attention to issues to watch out for. I also talk you through best practice in general when it comes to putting together your submission package, as well as discussing common pitfalls to be avoided by the debut writer.

My insider knowledge of the industry makes this book a useful tool even for those who have nearly completed their first work, but who are looking for advice on how to get the book published. I suggest resources for finding literary agents, and explain every aspect of the publishing process, from pitching your book to literary agents through to what happens when you get your first publishing deal. In a changing landscape, where more and more people are turning to self-publishing, it is important to remember that traditional publishing is not the only route to seeing your book in print. I mention some key resources for self-published authors, and look at the pros and cons of deciding to self-publish your novel. This section also contains information on 'hybrid' authors, those who choose to have some of their work traditionally published, while retaining the rights to self-publish others of their novels.

Get Started in Writing Young Adult Fiction also contains links to and suggestions for other resources for a writer to turn to: from online writing communities, to tips on how to find people to critique your work, and other books and websites which are designed to help a beginner novelist. Sometimes writing a novel can feel lonely, but the reality is that there are hundreds of thousands of writers out there, many of whom can offer you support. Some writers prefer to go it alone – but if you want to find people out there to help, you can, and this book will offer advice on how.

Through a mixture of easy-to-follow advice, writing exercises, industry insider knowledge and case studies, *Get Started in Writing Young Adult Fiction* will hold your hand through the unfamiliar world of creative writing for a young adult audience. By the end of the book you will have the skills – and the confidence – necessary to turn that daunting blank page into a polished and readable YA novel. If this book can help just one writer finish writing a book that they are proud of, I will feel that it has done its job well.

Key to the icons used in this book

 Snapshot exercise

 Write exercise

 Edit exercise

 Workshop exercise

 Key idea

 Focus point

1

Getting started

Rick Riordan, bestselling author of the Percy Jackson series

'"Harry Potter" opened so many doors for young adult literature. It really did convince the publishing industry that writing for children was a viable enterprise. And it also convinced a lot of people that kids will read if we give them books that they care about and love.'

The term 'young adult' (YA) was first used to describe certain works of literature by the Young Adult Library Services Association in the 1960s. The term was used to categorize books which were aimed at a readership aged 12–18.[1] Books such as *The Outsiders* by S.E. Hinton and the Nancy Drew series are examples of early young-adult fiction.

---

[1] Ashley Strickland, *A Brief History of Young Adult Literature*, CNN, http://edition.cnn.com/2013/10/15/living/young-adult-fiction-evolution/, Accessed 22 December 2014.

YA novels have undergone a renaissance in recent years. The success of titles in such series as Harry Potter, Twilight and The Hunger Games has seen much more investment and growth in publishing for teen readers. Other recent successes in this area have been books such as *The Fault in Our Stars*, *Eleanor & Park* and *Divergent*. These books are all very distinct from one another when it comes to style and genre, but they all share the quality of being appealing and believable to a younger readership. Rather than focusing on adults as their main characters, they deal with younger characters in a way which aims never to patronize or talk down to the readership.

This chapter will focus on helping you understand the different age ranges within children's publishing and how to figure out where your work sits. It will also look at word counts and teen genres to help you focus on who the audience for your work is going to be, and it will advise you on creating the best possible point of view for your YA novel. Many adult writers think that writing for a YA audience is somehow easier, but the opposite is true in my opinion. You have to tell a story in an interesting and page-turning way, while making sure that you keep a line between keeping the subject matter appropriate for the audience while never talking down to them. Many YA novels go on to become mainstream adult bestsellers as well, which shows how important it is to grasp this idea.

Understanding the Children's Book Consumer in the Digital Age is an ongoing biannual study from Bowker Market Research that looks at how children's book consumers are changing and developing. Their 2012 study showed that 55 per cent of buyers of YA works are aged 18 or older, and that people aged between 30 and 44 are responsible for 28 per cent of YA sales. This really hits the point home that when you are writing a YA book you are still dealing with complex ideas and language.[2]

---

[2] New Study, '55 per cent of YA Books Bought by Adults', *Publishers Weekly*, http://www.publishersweekly.com/pw/by-topic/childrens/childrens-industry-news/article/53937-new-study-55-of-ya-books-bought-by-adults.html, Accessed 22 December 2014

Know your audience

It is important to have an idea from the start of the audience and
age range you are writing for. Obviously, it is crucial that you tell the
story you want to tell, but an understanding of who you are telling
this story to is integral to successfully writing a YA novel. We will
look at the different age ranges in the children's market, to ensure
that you are targeting the correct one for the story you are trying to
tell.

Some people mistakenly label 'young adult' as a genre when it is
not a genre at all: it is about age categorization. Within the 'young
adult' umbrella you can find romance novels, fantasy novels, literary
novels and even crime novels. Many different genres are classed as
YA novels, because what they have in common is the age range of
the intended audience.

Age categories

There are many age categories used for children's fiction in general.
The youngest of these categories is board books, which are aimed
at children from newborn to aged three. The oldest category of
children's writing is crossover novels, which are designed to appeal
to adults as well as to children – these are sometimes referred to as
'new adult' novels. It is important to make sure that you are writing
for the age range you think you are writing for. Make sure that,
if you intend to write a YA novel, that you do not unintentionally
write a middle-grade novel.

Middle-grade novels are aimed at children aged 8–12. In other
words, they are pre-adolescents or a 'tween' audience. While it is OK

to not know the precise age of your audience (you do not need to be as specific as 'a 14-year-old girl living in Sussex'!) it is important to make sure that you are aware of the age bracket your book generally falls into. While middle-grade novels can still use fairly advanced vocabulary and language, they tend to be characterized by focusing on one major plot arc, with smaller subplots relegated to the background.

The themes are also an important consideration. Middle-grade novels tend not to feature very much romance, or if they do it is of the 'puppy love' variety. Rarely does it become a main focus of the story. Sex, drink and drugs do not tend to be part of the reality that the majority of pre-teens experience, so middle-grade novels generally shy away from these areas. The word count can also be expected to be lower: middle-grade novels tend to be a maximum of 45,000 words long.

The age of the character is also an important consideration. Most children will read up – so they will read about a character who is older than them – but they will rarely read down. If your main characters tend to be around the ten-year-old or eleven-year-old mark then there is a large chance that they are going to appeal to a middle-grade audience rather than a YA audience. It is also important that you do not write a character who is too old for characters to respond to: 13-year-olds are unlikely to relate to the concerns of a 30-year-old, for example.

While the focus of this book is on writing a YA novel, it is also useful to examine what 'new-adult' novels are. 'New-adult fiction' was a term first used by St Martin's Press in 2009 when they requested submissions of books which were designed to appeal to adults as well as older teenagers. They stated: 'We are actively looking for great, new, cutting-edge fiction with protagonists who are slightly older than YA and can appeal to an adult audience. Since twenty-somethings are devouring YA, St Martin's Press is seeking fiction similar to YA that can be published and marketed as adult—a sort of "older YA" or "new adult."'[3]

---

[3] St Martin's New Adult Contest, http://sjaejones.com/blog/2009/st-martins-new-adult-contest/, Accessed 22 December 2014

New-adult fiction is aimed at an 18- to 30-year-old audience, or a 'crossover' market. Some 'crossover' books will have book jackets intended for a younger audience, and separate book jackets designed for an adult audience.

Here are some examples of books which had an adult cover, as well as a cover aimed at a younger market:

- The Harry Potter series by J.K. Rowling (Bloomsbury)
- *Out of Shadows* by Jason Wallace (Andersen Press/Vintage)
- *Maggot Moon* by Sally Gardner (Hot Key Books)
- *The Hunger Games* by Suzanne Collins (Scholastic)
- *The Amber Spyglass* by Philip Pullman (Scholastic)
- *Eragon* by Christopher Paolini (Random House Children's Books).

The key way to distinguish new adult from young adult is by looking at the following: the age of the protagonist, the issues they face, and the prevalence of darker themes and more adult content. YA novels usually feature protagonists aged between 13 and 18, and typically these protagonists are still at school – the books do not follow them at university as the teen audience is not yet at that stage in their life. However, new-adult books feature protagonists aged 18 and up who may be moving away from home, starting their first job and becoming financially independent. Some new-adult fiction can also feature fairly graphic sex scenes. While YA novels do involve romance and often will deal with sex or sexual activity, this is rarely described in great detail. Some new-adult novels, such as *Slammed* by Colleen Hoover and *Easy* by Tamarra Webber, do feature graphic sexual content.

Key idea

Schools are a really popular setting in a lot of YA fiction. From the ballet school of Noel Streatfeild to *Vampire Academy*, school settings feel very familiar for a YA audience, and are perennially popular for the market.

Snapshot

Think back to when you were a YA reader. Write down six books which you remember reading and enjoying as a teenager. Answer the following questions about these books:

- How complex is the language used?
- How old are the protagonists in each book?
- What are the overarching themes of each novel?
- Do the novels have many subplots?

Aided with your new understanding of the differences between middle-grade and YA fiction, have a go at sorting the books by age, from youngest to oldest. Does this match with your own experience of how old you were when you first read them?

There are some books which defy these categorizations and become classics irrespective of age. However, for the vast majority of novels this categorization is a helpful tool which allows publishers to signpost your book for its intended audience. An awareness of novels which sit in the same category as yours is really helpful, and this understanding will give you a head start when submitting your book to agents. If you are sending middle-grade novels to agents who do not represent middle-grade novels, then you are immediately at a disadvantage.

Key idea

Understanding age categorizations will help you start to think like a professional writer and means that you will be communicating with the right audience from the start.

YA novels are aimed at children aged 12 and upwards. While adult readers – as discussed earlier – do also sometimes read them, the accepted cap for a YA readership is 18. The word count for YA novels can be much more fluid than in categories aimed at younger readers. Most are between 50,000 and 70,000 words, although word counts of 70,000-plus are not uncommon, especially in fantasy or science-fiction novels which feature complex worlds and detailed worldbuilding. In my own experience, the shortest YA novel I have sold to a publisher was 65,000 words and the longest was 100,000 words. A middle ground between these two is ideal, although it is important neither to pad out nor to rush through your plot just for the sake of word count – a subject we will discuss in a later chapter.

How old should my protagonist be?

YA novels should be told by YA voices. As discussed earlier, the age of the protagonist can make a big difference in the age of the audience who will read your book. Young readers will read up but very rarely read down, so it is important to get this right from the start.

One mistake which some writers make, when starting on a YA novel, is to have their novel narrated by an adult who is looking back on their past. This rarely works because applying adult perspectives to childhood experiences can create an uneven tone, and one which is unrealistic and unappealing to the intended audience. Some novels also feature mainly adult characters, or spend too much time focusing on the adult characters rather than the teen characters. I am often submitted YA books where the characters are all in their mid-twenties. The issues which affect people in their mid-twenties are very different from those which affect teenagers. Not handing in homework on time, not passing a test, not being asked out by the boy of your dreams to the school dance – these concerns are not going to affect the average grown-up! Teenagers like to read about people of their own age, or who are going through similar experiences to them. Few teenagers are financially independent or living away from home, so books which focus on adults can feel dull and uninspiring to a teen market.

Many YA novels have entirely absent parents – maybe because the book is set at a school or at a camp, or because the parents have been killed. While it isn't necessary for every author to not mention adults at all, be sure that adult voices and concerns aren't the main focus of your YA novel.

Similarly, it can also be a mistake to write a protagonist who is too young for your intended audience, or too young for the themes of your novel. If your novel is intended for 15-year-olds to read, then don't make it about a 12-year-old who is just starting at a new school. If you want to deal with dark themes, then make sure your main character would be old enough to experience them and to describe and understand them. If your book is about first love, then consider whether a 16-year-old protagonist would be more fitted to the book than a 12-year-old one.

Snapshot

Cast your mind back to when you were a teenager and write down three of the most important milestones you were preoccupied with – they could be going to big school, having your first kiss, or getting your first part-time job. How important do they seem to you now with the benefit of hindsight? If you wrote about them from the perspective of your current adult self, how might your tone differ from if you wrote about them from the perspective of yourself at that age?

Write

Write a paragraph about your thirteenth birthday. What were you given? Did you have a party? Do you remember what you wore that day? What did you most want? Did the day disappoint you? Now repeat this activity, but for your eighteenth birthday party. Read both pieces of work and identify how your concerns changed between 13 and 18. The gifts you wanted when you were 13 would have seemed childish to an 18-year-old. The clothes you wore as an 18-year-old would not have appealed to you as a 13-year-old. Remember that choosing the right age for your protagonist can be crucial to the success of your work, and how important it is that your protagonist feels believable.

A teenage character can look back on their younger years in a novel, but you cannot give them adult wisdom and hindsight, as this can result in a book which feels 'preachy'. The concerns of a grown-up won't impact on a YA audience: thinking that your book is concerned with things they cannot relate to makes it unlikely that they would pick it up to read. Some people struggle with whether their young protagonist means that their book is young adult. The key differential is that most adult books featuring young protagonists are written from an adult perspective, whereas those which are designed for a YA audience do not necessarily feature adult concerns, perspective or hindsight.

Genres

As we have already discussed, 'young adult' in and of itself is not a genre. However, it is a good idea to figure out what genre you are writing in within the YA umbrella. This will definitely help when you are targeting agents, and also when you are considering who exactly you envisage your audience to be. For example, a 13-year-old who likes novels with romance in is not going to be the natural audience for a book about a teenage spy trying to bring down a corrupt government. Understanding genres within YA fiction can really help when creating a compelling book – and help you know how to sell it.

There are many different YA genres and publishers will also be aware of these, and aware of particular trends. I would always recommend that you do not try to write for a particular trend, but instead concentrate on writing the story you want to tell. If sparkly vampire novels are performing particularly well and you decide to write one, by the time you are ready to submit to agents and to editors that particular trend will probably be over. It can also take 12 months from signing a deal for your book to hit the shelves, so that trend will probably be well and truly over! The best books also seem to start trends, rather than following them. No one expected wizarding novels to be big before Harry Potter. No one expected a book about a boy and his dragon to take off before Eragon. Great stories are timeless, so you should not allow yourself to be too constricted by what you think the market wants at a particular time.

Having said that, it is still useful to look at genres which are performing well (and badly) and to see where your own book sits within these. When you are submitting your book to agents and editors, or self-publishing it, you will be able to market your book in a more targeted way if you are aware of its genre. Is it a thriller?

Science fiction? A contemporary romance? An adventure novel? Knowing the genre you aim to write in can be a really good way of focusing the mind during the writing process and making you realize the kind of book you want to be writing.

Focus point

Some people can be snobbish about 'genre' fiction as opposed to 'literary' fiction but ultimately you should write the book you want to write: not the book you feel that you are supposed to write. No genre is 'bad' or 'good' – there are only individual books which can have differing levels of quality.

Margaret Atwood

'There is good and mediocre writing within every genre.'

Snapshot

Look at romance, fantasy and thrillers as a genre, and consider what defines them into those genres. Try to find at least one YA novel which fits into each of those categories. How can you tell? What difference do you think it makes to the way those books are marketed and who they are marketed to?

Points of view

One of the important things to consider is the point of view (POV) you will use when writing the novel. A lot of YA novels are written in the first-person POV. This has some obvious benefits: it lends an immediacy to the work and also allows us to get inside a character's head very quickly and to understand them from the start. Some writers believe that a first-person narrative really brings a book to life.

One example of this is with a client of mine, Liz de Jager. Liz's debut YA trilogy, which begins with *Banished*, was bought by Tor UK and the first book was published in 2014. The original draft of *Banished* was very different from the version I saw and signed. The biggest difference was that the original version had been written in the third person, and when it was initially rejected by agents, one mentioned that the voice was a problem. When Liz redrafted the book she wrote it in first-person present tense, which was not something she had tried in the past. As soon as she tried it in first-person present tense she felt that the story became faster and more immediate. It was this version of the novel which I signed, and this version which was ultimately published.

Ned Vizzini

'I always start a book thinking that it can be something other than first-person present, and I always come back to first-person present. It's just the easiest way.'

However, there are some things to be aware of when considering the POV of the novel. One main issue can be how restrictive first-person POV can be. If you are writing as one person and we are seeing the world through their eyes, it can be particularly difficult to introduce subplots. It can also be difficult to show the reader events which are happening 'off-camera'. For example, if *The Lord of the Rings* were told from Frodo's POV, we would be entirely restricted to where he went, who he spoke to, and what he saw. Because it is told in the third person, we can instead also be introduced to other settings, other perspectives of the war, and the fates of other characters that he could not know about. Some first-person POV narratives are deliberately unreliable, and thrive off turning the reader's expectations on their head. However, this can be a tricky thing for a writer to balance. How do you make the audience understand that the narrator is unreliable? How do you show that inconsistencies are deliberate rather than mistakes on your part?

Some authors use several different first-person POVs within a novel, rather than just one. This allows them to show different perspectives, and can also solve the problem of being restricted by what one character sees and feels. Introducing several voices allows you to bring different ideas to the table, as well as more complicated subplots. However, one problem of several POVs can be that the reader ends up skipping some of them. Inevitably, one or two of the POVs will be stronger and more convincing than the other(s) and you need to ask yourself if those other POVs are necessary, or if they are in fact slowing the story down for the reader.

Focus point

Sometimes it will take a while to get your POV right. Feel free to experiment. Try out writing in third person as well as first, and perhaps try writing from the point of view of a few different characters before you decide which one feels right. This is a personal thing, and can be the key to unlocking your novel, so take your time and try out different things.

Of course, there are other things to consider as well as whether you use first-person or third-person POV. Some writers choose to use 'close' third-person POV. This necessitates the writer – and the reader – entering the head of the protagonist, but still giving us more distance than if the book were written in first person. In first-person POV, as discussed, the POV character has to be present in every single scene, as discussed, but in third person – even close third person – you still leave yourself room to introduce other POVs. If you are going to use close third person and introduce other POVs, then great – just make sure that you don't flip back and forth too many times within a scene! It can be very confusing for the reader to be hearing about John's perspective on an argument only to suddenly be in Jane's shoes.

Write

Write a paragraph about your first day at senior school/high school. Write this firstly in first-person POV: 'I felt... I saw... I said...' Once you have completed this, go back and write it again in third-person POV.

Research

Would you trust a patisserie chef who never ate pastries? No, probably not. Similarly, I always distrust writers who do not read books in the area which they are writing in. The number-one tip I always give to writers is to read, read and do some more reading. This doesn't mean that you should be copying the ideas or styles of other authors, but what it does mean is that you should try to become a critical reader. Read the bestselling YA novels and the novels which are winning prizes. Go to your local library and ask the librarian what the most borrowed YA novels are. Also read YA novels which have had bad reviews, or which people have heavily criticized. Establish your own views on these.

Does the POV work? Does the language feel believable? Did you find the novel fast paced? Did you want to read on? If you disliked the book, it is also important to ask yourself why you disliked it. Was it a flaw with the characters? Did you not find it interesting? Was it confusing, or too simplistic? You will find that reading in a critical way will help you become a more critical writer as well. If you start to notice that too many characters have the same 'flaws', then make sure that your own main character does not have the same problem. If you find some novels are slowed down by too much dialogue, then ensure that this is not an issue in your own work. You will also start to discover what works for you in a positive way. You will see how fight scenes are structured, when novels make you laugh, and when you find yourself staying up late to read on. Some of these things will be unique to this novel, but many of them will not be. You can also try to utilize these tips and tricks in your own work.

Focus point

The best writers are also readers. Reading widely in the YA market will help you understand the competition, and where your own book might fit into it.

Tess Gallagher

'When you start reading in a certain way, that's already the beginning of your writing. You're learning what you admire and you're learning to love other writers. The love of other writers is an important first step. To be a voracious, loving reader.'

Edit

I want you to turn now to the exercise of writing POV earlier. I want you to pick which POV you felt worked best for the following criteria:
- pace
- voice
- story
- intrigue.

If you had to pick one to read on, which voice would it be in?

Which voice did you find easiest to write in? Why? Which voice do you think would most appeal to your intended audience?

Look again at your exercise of describing your birthday as a 13-year-old and as an 18-year-old.

- Does the voice feel believable?
- Would a teen reader respond to the concerns you have in each?
- Which is stronger?
- Which felt more natural to write?
- Which voice do you think you would find easier to sustain over an entire novel? Why?

Try rewriting both exercises paying particular attention to pace, voice, story and intrigue. Analyse which POV and which age feel most natural to you, and most natural to the story you are trying to tell.

Workshop

The following passage is some text I have written for the purpose of helping you understand how to try out different POVs to see which works best for you.

I was walking towards the bus stop when I first saw Bill McCourt. I'd heard about him, obviously – you can't be friends with Holly and not hear about anyone interesting, or weird, or whatever – but I'd never seen him, though I'd wondered if I'd bump into him before school started. He was shorter than she had said, and he looked more... normal I guess. Just a typical fifteen-year-old boy. I'd expected him to have some sign stamped on his forehead like I HAD AN AFFAIR WITH MY TEACHER AND SHE IS IN PRISON NOW. Though I guess that's a lot of words to fit on a forehead, isn't it? But still, he just stood there looking average. Brown hair, blue eyes, jeans, cons, same stuff all the other boys at St Chad's wear. He was fiddling with his phone, and ignoring everyone around him. Which was understandable, since the other girls from my school were huddling and whispering, even doing a bit of pointing, like, so subtle of them. We weren't supposed to know his name, or what he looked like, but Holly's mum's such a gossip and anyway you can never keep secrets in a town like ours. My parents hate how everyone knows everyone else's business but it's hard not to get sucked into it, no matter how hard you try to fight it you'll find you're caught up in it every day. Whose skirt was too short. Who was caught smoking behind the science block. Harmless stuff. But the stuff about Joe McCourt wasn't harmless, I guess, not if the tabloids were to be believed.

This passage is in first-person POV. I want you to answer the following questions about it:

- What do we learn about the narrator? Are they male or female? How old do you think they are? What other details do we know about them from the text?
- What information do we gain about the main character from this paragraph?
- Try transposing the paragraph into third-person POV. What was difficult about that? What information did you lose? How might you be able to convey that information in other ways?
- Using this exercise and your earlier exercises, analyse which feels most natural to you, and why? Which feels most like it will fit with your writing style?

Next step

In this chapter we have examined what the category young adult means and learned that 'young adult' is definitely not a genre. We have looked at subgenres within YA and what differentiates them from one another. We have also looked at how to identify your audience and how to understand the age range you are writing for, and to assess whether or not the themes you are considering will be appealing and appropriate to them. We have also assessed different POVs and tried out writing in different POVs: assessing the limitations of each, and what you gain and lose from a first- or third-person perspective. In the next chapter we are going to move on to ideas. How do you come up with ideas? And once you have an idea, how do you sustain it over an entire novel?

2

The big idea

In the last chapter we learned a lot about the background of the YA market, and the current young adult publishing sphere. We learned about preparing to write your novel, deciding on the POV and the age range you are targeting. In this chapter we are going to talk about ideas. Where do ideas come from, how do writers get their ideas, and how do you know if an idea has legs? We are also going to look at making sure that your idea is appropriate for a young adult audience. Finally, we'll look at originality and trends in ideas, and how to make sure your idea stands the test of time.

Looking at a blank piece of paper can seem incredibly daunting – how will you come up with an idea and, hardest of all, how will you make sure that it's a good one?

There are some really easy steps to make sure that you are in the best frame of mind for coming up with ideas. A good night's sleep, keeping hydrated and a 'writing station' are all helpful. That 'writing station' can simply be a laptop in a shed, or a notepad in your local library, but developing a routine around your writing can really help the creative juices flow. Some people swear by meditating: by clearing the mind, focusing on their breathing, and relaxing, loads of ideas bubble up to the surface.

But of course there is no one 'right' way of getting ideas. Ideas can also strike in the strangest of places: travelling on the tube, from a conversation with a co-worker, or just from reading an interesting news report or article. It is a really good idea to carry a notebook and pen around with you, or a phone, or laptop, or some way of jotting things down as and when they occur to you. You never know – that line about a funny-looking dog you just saw could easily turn into the opening of a novel! (Maybe not a bestselling one – but it is a start, at least.) However, some people find that when the best idea strikes them it is good for them to let it percolate rather than writing straight away. A famous example of this is of course J.K. Rowling, the author of the Harry Potter series.

 ## J.K. Rowling

'I was travelling back to London on my own on a crowded train, and the idea for Harry Potter simply fell into my head.

To my immense frustration, I didn't have a pen that worked, and I was too shy to ask anybody if I could borrow one...

I simply sat and thought, for four (delayed train) hours, while all the details bubbled up in my brain, and this scrawny, black-haired, bespectacled boy who didn't know he was a wizard became more and more real to me.

I began to write Philosopher's Stone *that very evening, although those first few pages bear no resemblance to anything in the finished book.'*

Key idea

Get into the habit of writing down interesting ideas which occur to you during the day. Who is that woman who always sits in the same seat on your bus? Why are that couple fighting? Become an interested observer of people and of your surroundings and become used to writing down these ideas, no matter how slight they may seem.

Key idea

Start keeping an 'ideas list'. For one week note down at least five ideas a day: they can be anything from a piece of dialogue you have heard to a stranger you have seen to a piece of news you saw which captured your imagination. At the end of the week you will have 35 ideas, which is a lot. Not all of them will be good, and you should not worry about every one of them being absolutely brilliant, but at least a few might well spark off interesting story ideas for you to develop.

Lots of writers have different ways of coming up with ideas, and different topics which sparked off their writing. Here are some examples of where novel ideas came from:

- C.S. Lewis was 16 years old when he had a bizarre daydream – that a half-man/half-goat creature was hurrying through snowy woods carrying an umbrella and a bundle of parcels. Years later, when he was 40, C.S. Lewis started to write about Tumnus the faun in *The Lion, the Witch and the Wardrobe*.

- Jessie Burton visited the Rijksmuseum in Amsterdam in 2009 and visited a dolls' house there which belonged to Petronella Oortman. The dolls' house was from the seventeenth century and had cost as much as a full-sized house. The image stuck with her and she began to write her debut novel, *The Miniaturist*.

- John Green's first inspiration for *The Fault in Our Stars* came from working as a student chaplain at a children's hospital. He was struck by the fact that these children, even though they were very ill, were still people – he wanted to create a story which showed their humanity and complexity.

- *Twilight* was inspired by a dream which the author, Stephenie Meyer, had. In her dream two people were having a conversation in a meadow. 'One of these people was just your average girl. The other person was fantastically beautiful, sparkly, and a vampire. They were discussing the difficulties inherent in the facts that A) they were falling in love with each other while B) the vampire was particularly attracted to the scent of her blood, and was having a difficult time restraining himself from killing her immediately.'[1]

As you can see, writers can have their imagination sparked by many different things – from an advert to an artefact. Some find that the first line of their novel springs fully formed into their head and they write it down, and find their way through the rest of the story. Ideas can strike at any time, you just need to take notice of them. That is why it is a good idea to get used to writing them down when they strike you in an ideas book, or an ideas document. You can quickly discard some of the ideas as not helpful, but some of them will stick with you when you go back to look at them again.

 ## Mary Shelley, *Frankenstein*

'I placed my head on my pillow, I did not sleep, nor could I be said to think. My imagination unbidden, possessed and guided me, … I saw with shut eyes, but acute mental vision, – the pale student of unhallowed arts standing before the thing he had put together, I saw the hideous phantasm of a man stretched out, and then, on the working of some powerful engine, show signs of life and stir with an uneasy, half vital motion…'

Your brain is an amazing piece of equipment, and you will find that you have a lot of ideas nestled in there – you just need to find the way to tap into them. One good way of coming up with ideas is brainstorming. Often, people think that brainstorming is purely a

---

[1] Stephenie Meyer, 'The Story behind Twilight', http://stepheniemeyer.com/twilight.html, Accessed 22 December 2014.

group activity, but you can actually brainstorm really effectively on your own. Simply grab a blank sheet of paper and start writing any ideas you can down on the page.

Snapshot

Get a blank sheet of paper and brainstorm the following topics, coming up with as many ideas as you can in five minutes for each:

- my favourite food
- things that annoy me
- countries I want to visit
- my family
- things I hate.

Of course, you can also brainstorm around a theme. Say you have decided to write a novel about teens struggling with divorcing parents, you could choose to brainstorm solely around this topic and see what you come up with. Some ideas will quickly prove themselves to be dead ends, but some ideas will prove to have longevity. You will find that the more you focus on the ideas which have depth, the more you can write.

Key idea

Some ideas can end up trapping you in a corner. We hear a lot about 'hooks' and high-concept novels: sometimes these can be great, but sometimes that million-dollar idea can actually trap you. The idea of a world in which humans live underwater and are at war with fish could seem really cool – until you start writing it and realize that the backstory makes no sense and you really have only a few hundred words of interesting material. Do not be afraid to play around with ideas, and to dispose of those which trap you: the best ideas will free you rather than feeling restrictive.

Free writing

One way of coming up with ideas is to try free writing. Free writing is a technique which is used by many writers as a warm-up exercise before they start writing properly for the day. The idea behind free writing is that it allows the writer to loosen up their mind and begin to allow the ideas to flow, helping the writer lose their inner doubts and tap into their inner stream of consciousness.

The exercise takes place for a set period of time – normally anywhere up to 30 minutes – and you should write continuously with no regard to spelling, grammar, or even staying on the same topic. You are not supposed to edit the work either, but should just keep writing rather than going back over and over the text. One of my bestselling writers refers to this as 'word vomit', which is a rather unpleasant image but one which perfectly encapsulates the idea behind it. If you cannot come up with anything to write about, you should simply write 'I cannot think of anything to write about' until something else comes to mind! The other rule is that you cannot judge yourself or critique yourself as you write: your job is to simply set words down on paper during the time frame and then look at them.

Once the free-writing exercise is over, the writer has a free-flowing, perhaps misspelled, paragraph. Writers can use it in different ways. Some find that it is a way of cleaning out the mind, before starting more focused, serious writing. Others can use it as a way to spark off ideas which they will then give more time and attention to during the writing process.

Free writing has several key benefits. These include helping you get over the hurdle of staring at a blank page, helping you switch off that inner critical voice that paralyses your writing process, and – this is a key one – helps you come up with ideas and discover topics to write about. Do not think before you start writing; simply sit down and start letting the words flow.

It is also possible to try free writing based around a particular topic, or topics, rather than whatever springs to mind. You can try free writing around any number of ideas to see what ends up on the page.

There are other simple ways you can start coming up with ideas for your novel. Maybe nine out of ten of them won't be of any use, but if even one of them is, it's worth taking the time to come up with these ideas. Many writers find that reading other novels is a good place to start. We've already talked about the importance of reading critically, but what about the importance of spotting other interesting ideas through writing? Many books, when you boil them down, encompass a handful of themes – a battle between good and evil, a coming-of-age story, the pain of first love, or a quest. The same is true of films and plays. Reading widely, but also watching plays, listening to radio shows or watching classic films can also help you discover what it is that is interesting about their ideas and themes.

Truman Capote

> *'Writing has laws of perspective, of light and shade just as painting does, or music. If you are born knowing them, fine. If not, learn them. Then rearrange the rules to suit yourself.'*

Universal themes, unique perspectives

Lots of writers find that they feel most comfortable writing from experience. 'Write what you know' is a famous expression, and something a lot of writers live by. Drawing experiences from your own life means that you can imbue them with a depth you might not otherwise achieve, and it certainly means you will never be lacking for inspiration. However, it is important to make sure that, even if the story is personal to you, it can be universal in appeal.

I worked with an author whose novel was directly inspired by her own childhood experience one summer when she was 16. As the writing progressed, I felt that, while her story was great, it was too personal to her, which limited the story's appeal. It felt 'too quiet', as if the story was too tightly linked to her own life and experiences which might not have the same resonance for other readers. We worked hard to make sure that, even though the novel was inspired by her life, this did not become a noose around her neck, and that the book could also appeal to people who were very different to her. By changing some of the experiences of the character and creating more dramatic events, the book began to feel less like memoir and more like a novel.

Often, you can use the lens of your own experience to widen an idea into something much more universal. The story of the death of your dog, your first kiss or your first day at school might seem unique to you, but if you focus on the emotions underpinning these experiences they can become much more widely appealing. The best stories are a mixture of unique (your dog was a collie, and he died on your thirteenth birthday) and universal (how does first loss impact on a teenager's life?).

Snapshot

Write a couple of paragraphs about the death of your first pet. Focus on blending the specific – the pet's name, how it happened – with the universal themes of grief and loss.

Edit

I now want you to go back to the earlier free-writing exercise. Go through it adding proper punctuation and grammar. Now evaluate whether there are any ideas which might actually prove interesting to work on. Are there any sentences which stand out? Are there any common themes which you seem to be dealing with?

Focus point

The best novels contain at least something of their writer's experience. Maybe you have never been a teenage mercenary fighting for a rebel government – but you can still bring your unique experience to bear in the way the character deals with growing up, or first love, or grief and loss. Blend your unique experience with a universal theme to create the strongest story.

Maggie Harcourt, YA novelist

'A friend once told me that the most important thing in a YA book – *any* YA book – from a writer's point of view is honesty. It doesn't matter what your story is, or who's in it, or even how it ends… as long as you're honest. It isn't about trying to write for an audience and it isn't about trying to lecture or second-guess. You can't have an agenda or go into it wanting to stay "on message". One thing all the great YA books I've read have in common is their emotional honesty: be fearless, and see where it takes you.'

Originality

Sometimes it can feel like all of the good ideas have been taken already! And there are definitely certain themes and ideas which pop up time and time again in literature, and which have universal appeal. Ideas such as first love, first loss, coming-of-age, bullying, good vs evil and a quest pop up again and again in novels. However, it's how they are dealt with which differentiates them and gives a book a wider appeal. For example, there are a lot of books about orphans discovering they have special powers – but it doesn't seem to stop the books becoming successful!

Let's look at some examples where the same themes are used, but in a very different way:

- **Bullying:** *Harry Potter*, *The Perks of Being a Wallflower*, *Blubber*, *Divergent*
- **First love:** *Twilight*, *Forever*, *The Fault in Our Stars*, *Eleanor & Park*
- **Good vs evil:** *Code Name Verity*, *The Hunger Games*, *Noughts & Crosses*

While these novels contain some universal themes, what you can see is that they differ wildly from one another. This can be in setting, in tone, in language, and in characters. These novels use the same or similar ideas as a jumping-off point but then take the book in a completely different way.

When I first received *The Fire Sermon* by Francesca Haig on submission, in early 2013, it would have been easy to dismiss it as just another dystopian novel. There are a lot of YA novels set in a post-apocalyptic future, with a female lead. However, several things set this world apart from others. Even though it was a post-apocalyptic world, it was set so far in the future that technology no longer existed, immediately making it very different from novels such as *Divergent* and *The Hunger Games*. Secondly, the plot itself took lots of common themes, but reworked them into something completely fresh and new. In the novel, when anyone gives birth they give birth to twins: one 'alpha', whole and perfect, and one 'omega', who has a disability. When the omega is discovered they are branded and separated, as they live in an apartheid-like society. But when one twin dies, it kills the other. The book contained lots of common themes such as rebellion against the government, fight between good and evil, post-apocalyptic world, but blended them into something which felt wholly different. It was sold to 26 publishers around the world, and Dreamworks optioned the film rights.

Key idea

Humanity has been telling the same stories for centuries. Not every story is going to be completely new and original, but it needs to have enough originality to capture your readership's attention and make them want to read your book.

One good exercise for coming up with ideas is to look at existing novels and plot synopses, and to change one element about them, and then see how that might change the novel entirely. Think how different *Harry Potter* might have been if Harry was a girl. Imagine how *Twilight* might have changed if Bella had been the vampire rather than Edward. How might *The Hunger Games* read if Katniss was fighting alongside her sister, rather than her love interest. These are all small changes, but actually, they integrally change the face of the story. Changing the setting, the gender, the race, the world can all tip a story on its head and make what might seem a tired idea suddenly come to life.

Snapshot

Reimagine these blurbs for novels by changing one small detail about the book. Try changing the gender of the main characters, or the setting, or their conflict.

Carrie by Stephen King

Carrie White is no ordinary girl.

Carrie White has the gift of telekinesis.

To be invited to Prom Night by Tommy Ross is a dream come true for Carrie – the first step towards social acceptance by her high school colleagues.

But events will take a decidedly macabre turn on that horrifying and endless night as she is forced to exercise her terrible gift on the town that mocks and loathes her...[2]

Divergent by Veronica Roth

In the world of Divergent, society is divided into five factions and all are forced to choose where they belong. The choice Beatrice Prior makes shocks everyone, including herself.

Once decisions are made faction members are forced to undergo extreme initiation tests with devastating consequences. Tris must determine who her friends are – and whether the man who both threatens and protects her is really on her side.

Because Tris has a deadly secret. As growing conflict threatens to unravel their seemingly perfect society, this secret might save those Tris loves... or it might destroy her.[3]

City of Bones by Cassandra Clare

Sixteen-year-old Clary Fray is an ordinary teenager, who likes hanging out in Brooklyn with her friends. But everything changes the night she witnesses a murder, committed by a group of teens armed with medieval weaponry. The murderous group are Shadowhunters, secret warriors dedicated to driving demons out of this dimension and back into their own. Drawn inexorably into a terrifying world, Clary slowly begins to learn the truth about her family – and the battle for the fate of the world.[4]

 Key idea

Don't get overly hung up on whether your story idea feels completely original. Society has been telling the same stories for generations – and with one small twist, and with skilled writing, even old themes can feel fresh and new.

---

[2] Stephen King, *Carrie* (Hodder Paperbacks, 2013).

[3] Veronica Roth, *Divergent* (HarperCollins, 2014).

[4] Cassandra Clare, *City of Bones* (Walker Books, 2007).

Sometimes there can be traction in turning a book idea on its head; on taking an old, tired idea and flipping it so it becomes something totally different. A great example of this is the television show *Buffy the Vampire Slayer*. The creator, Joss Whedon, said he was struck by the fact that so many TV shows/films/books had pretty blonde teenage girls being preyed upon by monsters. He imagined what might happen if that pretty, blonde cheerleader was actually the thing the monsters were afraid of? In Buffy he created a relatable teen character – but by flipping on its head the idea of her as victim, he made the show feel fresh and new. There can also be traction in telling a book from an antagonist's perspective. The YA novel *Before I Fall* by Lauren Oliver is about a girl killed in a car crash who must live the same day over until she gets it right. The protagonist is the stereotypical 'mean girl': selfish and unkind. However, Oliver still makes you root for her, and her growth through the novel as she relives this day gives the book a lot of depth.

Imagine how different your favourite books might be if you wrote them from the POV of the villain instead. How would *Harry Potter* read if told from Draco Malfoy's POV? What would be challenging about writing a novel from the villain's perspective?

The Helsinki Bus Station theory

One of my favourite theories about the creative process is focused on the art world, although it applies wonderfully also to the novel-writing process, and deals with coping with originality of ideas – or lack thereof. It was first outlined in a 2004 graduation speech by Arno Minkkinen, and it is known as 'the Helsinki Bus Station theory'. The theory tells the artist to 'stay on the bus' at all costs. There are two dozen platforms, Minkkinen explains, and the buses at each platform take the same route out of the city and at first each bus makes identical stops along the way. So the traveller picks their direction – or the novelist their idea – and sets off along the bus route. However, a few stops down the line someone asks them 'but haven't you seen this work?' and you discover that that work shares similarities to your own. You presume that you are going to end up in the same place as every other passenger, so you get off the bus, get in a taxi and head back to the station, only to get on another bus route. But again, after a few stops, the same question is asked and you are back to square one.

The answer is to stay on the bus. Minkkinen explains that after the beginning, when the journeys are identical, the bus routes then start to go in different directions and to different destinations, and that is when the artist finds their unique vision. You have to commit to feeling as if you are treading over old ground in order to ride it out and create something truly unique.[5]

It is also important to consider whether the ideas you are coming up with fit in with the age you are planning on writing for. It's no good writing a novel about a boy entering the astronaut programme at aged 18 if your book is intended for 12-year-olds. Ask yourself what is important to children at that age. If you have children yourself who are teenagers, ask them what their main concerns are, and what their biggest issues might be. If not, ask a friend to ask their children the same question.

Go to the library and look at reference books aimed at young adults. Try reading non-fiction books which are aimed at 12-year-olds, and then at 16-year-olds – see the difference in language and in the topics being covered. A non-fiction book aimed at 12-year-olds which deals with sex will be very different to one aimed at 16-year-olds. Make sure that you are using age-appropriate topics and concerns for your audience.

A teenager of 16 is able to think about sex in a way which a 12-year-old won't be – and that 12-year-old probably won't want to be thinking about sex! As readers grow up, they are able to deal with reading about more complex issues and to understand them and process them. You need to make sure that your writing speaks to the age you are writing for, and that it won't patronize or confuse them.

One good way to start to understand this audience, as well as reading widely in fiction and non-fiction, is to watch the TV shows aimed at them and to read teenage magazines. It can be really difficult to put yourself in the mindset of a teenager and one of the most common issues I see in submissions is that they feel patronizing, or like they are talking down to their audience. They

---

[5] Oliver Burkeman, 'This Column Will Change Your Life: Helsinki Bus Station Theory', http://www.theguardian.com/lifeandstyle/2013/feb/23/change-life-helsinki-bus-station-theory, Accessed 22 December 2014.

are perhaps overly concerned with what adults *think* teenagers should be concerned with, rather than what they actually are going to be concerned with! Reading teen magazines and watching teen TV shows and films can help you understand what are the big concerns for teenagers, and what really makes them tick.

I am used to public speaking for my job, but whenever I speak to teenagers I have to tailor my speech for them. Adults will be polite when they are bored: teenagers will not. Adults will laugh at some jokes which teenagers won't get and vice versa. Sometimes the clever references which meant a lot to you as a teenager will be lost on a modern audience. Using out-of-date references, referring to TV shows which are out of favour, or even social networks which teenagers are no longer using can immediately make a book feel outdated. Of course, that isn't true of every book – books such as *The Catcher in the Rye* have stood the test of time, even though they are from a different age. But in general terms, making sure that your book feels believable for the teenagers who are going to be reading it is integral.

Some ideas won't feel appropriate for your target market when you revisit them. An idea about a spy in Cold War Russia might suddenly seem not so appropriate to a teenage audience. Sometimes, ideas run away from you, so the idea you think you are going to write morphs into something completely different. Your novel about a disfigured boy fighting back against bullies might suddenly change into a story about yearning and the discovery of first love. Make sure, while you are developing your ideas, that you always consider whether or not what you are writing is appropriate for its audience.

In my experience, YA writers don't often deal with inappropriate themes for their audience. But what I do see is that writers worry that their audience won't be able to cope with the themes and begin to write down to them. I asked one of my authors, Maggie Harcourt, author of *The Last Summer of Us* (Usborne) what the best advice I gave her was. Her novel is about a young girl dealing with the death of her mother, and I felt that emotional honesty was key. Maggie said 'You told me it felt like I was pulling my punches, and I shouldn't. I figure if this is true for me it will be true for other YA writers!' Remember that teenagers understand sophisticated concepts and ideas. If you are writing for a 12-year-old audience, you will need to have some awareness of what you are dealing with and how you are phrasing it, but if you are writing for an upper-end

YA novel then you don't need to pull your punches – they are sophisticated readers and nothing turns them off more than a book which feels like it is talking down to them!

Focus point

Remember that teen novels often deal with really dark subject matter. Novels such as *Speak*, which deals with the aftermath of a brutal sexual assault, or *Monster,* which is about a teenage boy on trial for his life, are not light reads. But they contain an emotional truth which resonates with their readership. These books are successful because they do not patronize the teen reader: they speak to them on a level.

Write

Get out your writing notebook and have a look at the list of 35 ideas you came up with. I want you to pick your favourite idea from the list. This idea could be anything from a news report you saw to a painting you looked at in a museum. Once you have picked your favourite idea, I want you to construct the opening to a novel based around it. While you are writing it, ask yourself if the story is interesting, if it is unique and universal, if it is different, and if it will be appealing to the age of reader you want to read it. You should aim for around 750 words for the piece. Don't get hung up on your first line or who your characters will be; just focus on creating an interesting opening to a book.

A big message

Sometimes writers feel the need to educate their readership through their work. If they feel passionately about an issue, sometimes they seek to use their fiction to convince their readership to feel the same way. Books which are about religion, about sex, about drugs, or about the environment can all perform well. The trick is, however, to not feel as if you are labouring the point or being too moralistic. As we have discussed already, it is important that your audience does not feel as though they are being patronized. They are intelligent enough to make their own decisions, so it is important not to be too heavy-handed. By all means talk about the issues which mean a lot to you, but make sure that you do so in a way which still allows the reader to make their own choices and decisions. Don't feel as if you have to hammer the point home on every page, as this is a sure-fire way to stop the story becoming interesting! Don't let the reader feel as if they are being lectured. My most hated books at school were those where I felt as if the lesson was being shoved down my throat – it was a quick way to make me ignore the lesson, if anything. You can have a moral message, but make sure that it is subtly woven through the book.

Knowledge

Sometimes the best ideas come from subjects you already know something about. If you are a deep-sea diver, a passionate horse-rider, or studied a particular period of history, it makes sense to tell a story which involves some of these elements. This is great if the ideas you come up with happen to fall within the remit of your knowledge. If you are a deep-sea diver and your story idea is about a boy learning to dive then that is wonderful, well done you. But what if you come up with a story idea that is nothing to do with any of your areas of knowledge? What do you do then?

My biggest piece of advice to you in this case is to educate yourself, and to research. One of the greatest problems with some novels is that it becomes clear that the author knows nothing – or very little – of what they are writing about. Sometimes people set novels in a part of the world where they have never visited, but it becomes clear that they have also done nothing more than a cursory Wikipedia-ing of the topic. I have read otherwise good books which are let down by a lack of research. What if you are American but setting your book in the UK? You need to know what types of school there are, if people might wear uniforms, what exams they would take at what age. If you choose to have your characters competing in national athletics competitions, then you need to research what they might expect from competing, how many in a squad, what results they would expect. There is no point being lazy once you have found an interesting idea.

Once you have found a good idea, write a list of questions you need to look into discovering the answers to. These can be as straightforward as when would they take their exams and what books might they study, or as complicated as what career might someone have in Brazil, or what was the life expectancy in Tudor England. Sometimes, once you have started writing, you will discover that you don't know the answers to things you were unaware of – don't ignore these but leave markers in the text reminding yourself to go and look that up!

With fantasy novels you have the luxury of being able to make things up more than in other novels, but of course one of the key rules of fantasy novels is: your world must be consistent and there must be rules. You can have dragons, or magic powers, or people who can fly, but we need to know the rules for what the dragons can do, when the magic powers work, and why people can fly.

Workshop

In an earlier snapshot exercise you looked at your favourite idea from the ideas list you kept for a week. You wrote a creative work inspired by this idea: the opening to a novel. Now go back and take a closer look at this piece of writing. I want you to look at the writing piece and answer the following questions about it:

- Is the opening interesting?
- Would you read on?
- Is the opening appropriate to your readership?
- Is the idea universal and unique? How so?
- Is the idea honest? Do you pull your punches?
- Do you know enough about the idea to carry the story on?
- Is the idea big enough to carry on for a novel?
- Did you feel constrained by the idea or inspired by the idea?
- Do you find the idea exciting?

I want you to write a few paragraphs 'reviewing' your own opening, as if it were written by someone else. You do not have to be too critical here, but it helps to be honest about what works and what doesn't. Would the story be interesting to 16-year-olds? If not, what could you do to address that? Do you have enough knowledge to carry the story on? If not, how could you do the necessary research to change this?

Once you have done this, *either* go back and revise your opening, fixing the issues you have spotted, *or* go back and write a new opening, having picked one of your other ideas. Make sure that you ask yourself throughout if it is original, universal, interesting and relatable to your audience. These are questions you will need to carry with you throughout the novel-writing process.

Next step

Now that you have learned how to come up with ideas and chosen one which interests you (and written your opening for a novel!), we are going to move on to planning a novel. You will learn whether you are a 'pantser' or a 'plotter' and what this means. You will learn the basic art of constructing a story. You will look at plot and action. These skills are integral to turning something from 750 words to a long-form, interesting novel.

3

Planning your novel

In this chapter we are going to look at how you should go about planning your novel before you begin to write it. So you have researched your market, you have come up with an idea, and you have done your basic research. Now what? How do you turn that idea, or ideas, into a 60,000-word-plus piece of writing? This part of the proceedings can be incredibly daunting. Some people find the ideas part of the process the easy bit, and even setting down those first few chapters is not too difficult – but how do you turn a short story into a substantial novel? What are the common pitfalls and how can you avoid them? In this chapter we will look at how to plan and structure a novel. We will look at how to juggle subplots and your main plot. We will also look at the common obstacles and how you can avoid them. By the end of this chapter you will be well on your way to knowing how to sustain your idea, and how to give it a gratifying and exciting plot throughout.

W. Somerset Maugham

'There are three rules for writing the novel. Unfortunately, no one knows what they are.'

Planning a novel sounds daunting, and some writers do not really like to do it. In fact, there are unofficial terms used to describe the two different types of novelist: plotters and 'pantsers'. Plotters are those writers who sit down before they start their novel and painstakingly plot out every aspect. This plotting can be as simple as a rough overview of where the novel is going, or as precise as a sentence describing what must take place in every chapter of the work. 'Pantsers', on the other hand, have a vague idea in their head of where they want the novel to go, but they 'fly by the seat of their pants', hence the name. They know roughly what the story will be but often go off on different tangents and in different directions. There is no one correct way to be – as you will find with so much writing advice you are given – as different ways of doing things suit some people better than others, and it is pointless to force yourself into behaving a certain way when it just does not come naturally to you.

However, in my opinion, when you are starting out as a writer it is a good idea to sit down and at least give yourself some idea of where you are going. Writing a novel is a tricky thing to do, especially when you have not done it before. Think of it as making a casserole without a recipe to guide you. With the recipe in place, you can still add different spices or amend things, but you know that you will end up in the place you meant to end up. If you cook without a recipe, you might have far too much flour, not enough meat, and create something not very satisfying to eat.

It is, of course, OK to experiment with novels, and with the novel-writing process, but having an idea of where your novel is going and how you are going to get there is essential to creating a gripping narrative.

Key idea

Think of the planning stage of the novel as like Theseus with the ball of string, leading himself out of the Labyrinth. Sometimes the ideas are coming thick and fast, or the writing is taking you in directions you never expected. What you need is a planning document, much like that ball of string, which will lead you out of the maze.

It is a great idea to become more aware of plots and structures in general, and to start to figure out precisely how they work and why exactly they work. Every time you watch a film, every time you read a book, or hear a fairy tale or a myth, try to analyse the story structure. Ask yourself if it worked, or if it didn't work. If it worked, why? If it didn't work, why not?

Snapshot

Look at two popular fairy tales and summarize what the plots were, and how the structures worked. Summarize the plots themselves in a couple of sentences, but also look at the structures too. Who were the main characters? Who was the antagonist? What was the main conflict? How was the story resolved? When was the conflict introduced? Was the story satisfying? Becoming a critical reader and being more aware in general of how plots and structure work can really help when you are developing your own plot and structure.

Titles

One of the best ways to start a novel is to come up with a title, or at least to come up with a working title: a title can sometimes help encapsulate your ideas and help you figure out what the plot is about. Coming up with a title is the first building block to planning your novel. Even if the title changes by the end, or you think of it as a working title if nothing else, deciding on what to call the book should lend framework and structure to your work. It should also help you crystallize your ideas.

Fantasy author Den Patrick's debut novel started with the title *The Boy with the Porcelain Ears*. His girlfriend at the time commented that his ears were 'so pale they looked like porcelain'. This struck him as an interesting book title and he began to think further around the idea. 'I knew there was an orphan, I knew it took place in a huge castle (thank you, Mervyn Peake) and I knew the King was a recluse. The orphan had porcelain ears because he lacked ears of his own. I'd always known this, but now other ideas occurred. What other deformities did he have, and were there other orphans like him? And were they pitted against each other and for what reason?'

The more questions he posed for himself, the more the writing flowed, and within eight months he had a 90,000-word-long novel. The publisher eventually changed the title, but it was that initial title idea that sparked off the book idea, and which also helped spark off the key questions and conflict that shaped the rest of the novel.

Coming up with a title can be an extremely useful exercise in focusing the mind on what the novel is about. One of the ways I suggest authors go about coming up with titles is by brainstorming the key themes of the novel, and then experimenting with words to do with these themes. Sometimes we also look at the settings of the novel, the characters, or the key conflict of the novel, and brainstorm ideas about these too.

Perhaps your novel is all about the idea of secrecy so you could brainstorm words around secrecy, keeping secrets, hiding away, or hiding things. Brainstorming ideas around a key concept can also be a useful way to decide on a title, so if your book is about dressmaking you could look at words around sewing, or mending. If it is historical fiction, maybe you could look at slang from the time. Quotes are also a popular way to title novels. The best titles are evocative and interesting.

Here are some of my favourite titles:
- *I Capture the Castle*
- *The Fault in Our Stars*
- *The Perks of Being a Wallflower*
- *Angus, Thongs and Full-frontal Snogging*
- *The Knife of Never Letting Go*
- *The Sisterhood of the Travelling Pants*

Getting to the heart of it

Once you have your working title, you need to come up with a one-sentence summary which encapsulates the plot. You've had your ideas, but now you need to sum up what you want to accomplish, or the experience which the reader will get from your novel. Normally this sentence will follow this pattern:

CHARACTER in SETTING must experience CONFLICT before CONCLUSION

Have a look at your ideas. Have you decided on your protagonist or protagonists? What is the world you are planning on setting your novel in? What is the conflict the characters will have to overcome? What do you want them to have achieved by the ending?

These ideas can be broad, sweeping and incredibly dramatic; or they can be smaller and quieter. Your conflict could be saving an empire, or navigating high school. Your conclusion could be them marrying a princess, or winning a talent competition.

Here are some examples of famous novels summed up in a sentence:

THE CURIOUS INCIDENT OF THE DOG IN THE NIGHT-TIME BY MARK HADDON

Fifteen-year-old Christopher Boone's suburban world is turned upside down when his next-door neighbour's poodle is murdered: but he must cope with his fear of the outside world and new people in order to get to the bottom of the mystery.

- The CHARACTER is 15-year-old Christopher Boone.
- The SETTING is suburbia.
- The CONFLICT is coping with his autism.
- The CONCLUSION is finding out what happened to his next-door neighbour's poodle.

THE PERKS OF BEING A WALLFLOWER BY STEPHEN CHBOSKY

Freshman Charlie is a sensitive teenager living in suburban Pittsburgh; can he deal with the secret traumas of his past in order to make friends and get through his first year of high school?

- The CHARACTER is freshman Charlie, a sensitive boy.
- The SETTING is Pittsburgh, and Charlie's high school.
- The CONFLICT is the secret traumas of his past.
- The CONCLUSION is Charlie making it through his first year of high school unscathed.

As you can see, these books are very different, but in describing them we can make them follow the 'CHARACTER in SETTING experiences CONFLICT to reach CONCLUSION' method.

 Snapshot

Write a sentence which condenses your own novel idea into one sentence. This sentence should introduce us to the main CHARACTER, the SETTING of the novel, the main CONFLICT, and lead us through to the CONCLUSION of the novel. It can be really hard to condense the idea to one sentence, but it is a really good discipline to get into – and it is also a really good lesson to learn for when pitching your novel, which we will move on to in a later chapter.

Developing your idea

Coming up with just one sentence is the hardest part of the process, and from this starting point, it becomes a lot easier to expand your idea. Once you have come up with this one sentence then it is a good idea to give yourself more space to detail each of those main areas. Have a think about your character, or characters. Who is the protagonist of your novel? Who is the antagonist of your novel? What is the setting of your novel? Sometimes the setting is straightforward and simple. It could be a contemporary novel set in a small seaside town, for example. But sometimes, the setting can be really complicated and you might need to consider this in more detail. The next stage is to jot down a few ideas about your main conflict: what form will it take, who will be involved? Finally, look at your resolution. How do you want the novel to end, what do you want your characters to have learned and experienced? Some endings don't need a finite, precise resolution, but the reader needs to feel satisfied by what you have given them.

The five Ws and H

The five Ws and H are traditionally used by journalists when investigating a story but can be incredibly useful to keep in mind when learning how to plot out your novel. You need to ask yourself the following questions about your story:

- **Who** is it about?
- **What** happened?
- **Where** did it happen?
- **When** did it take place?
- **Why** did it happen?
- **How** did it happen?

By answering these questions – in a straightforward, factual way – you can help build up a much clearer picture of where your story is going and how you are going to end it. It requires you to analyse your main cast of characters, tell us what happened, where it happened when it took place, why and how. Of course, this exercise does not cover everything that takes place in a novel, but it does require you to start thinking critically about your ideas and where you plan to take them.

Snapshot

Take the sentence you have used as a summary and work on developing this into a more detailed plan. For each heading (character/setting/conflict/conclusion) come up with at least five bullet points giving more information on each. This will be the blueprint for your novel. Well done – this is a big step forward in the writing process!

The rule of three

Stories should have a beginning, a middle and an end. This sounds obvious but sit down and think about what it really means for your novel. Is your idea big enough to sustain over these three acts?

THE BEGINNING (THE FIRST ACT)

This is typically 25 per cent of the novel in length. This should introduce your characters and setting and introduce the main *conflict*. The first act should also feature an inciting incident. This beginning should not be exposition heavy but you need to focus on the protagonist, the setting, and set up the main conflict or the main problem that the protagonist needs to solve. By the end of the first act the protagonist should be on the journey which will lead us to the end of the novel. You are setting up A and need to understand how it will lead to B.

The inciting incident is what kicks off the plot of the novel, taking us from the setting and basic reality you have established, into a stage of heightened tension. The inciting incident is really what kick-starts your story, and gets your readers focused on the plot, and on why they are reading your novel. An inciting incident is where we introduce the conflict of the novel. An inciting incident needs to happen in the early stages of the novel, as readers will expect something like this to happen early on in order to maintain their interest in the book.

For example, if your novel is about a boy who feels lost and alone, then the inciting incident could be discovering that his parents are not his real parents, and that he was adopted.

Here are some examples of inciting incidents from famous films and novels:

- *Divergent* The main character discovers that she is 'divergent' and therefore a threat to the rest of her society.
- *Monsters, Inc.* A human child enters into Monstropolis.
- *The Wizard of Oz* A tornado takes Dorothy away into a magical land.

THE MIDDLE (THE SECOND ACT)

This is typically 50 per cent of the novel in length. The action needs to be kicked up a notch here, and the protagonist should be trying to resolve the conflict that was introduced by the inciting incident. However, typically the conflict is just worsening. There should be a climax at the end of the second act.

In Act II we have already had the inciting incident (so the protagonist discovers he is adopted) but here we need give the character a *choice* of what to do with this information. We then need to introduce the complications that the protagonist has to overcome, we further deepen the characterization, and the clashes between the protagonist and the antagonist will take place.

For our protagonist searching for his birth mother in Act II, we would see him decide to investigate who his real mother is, argue with his adoptive family who don't want him to find her, struggle with the research necessary to discover her, and meet her, only for her to reject him.

During the middle the protagonist will often reach their lowest point and it will seem as if they are going to give up. Sometimes they do give up. But, hopefully, not for long!

THE END (THE THIRD ACT)

This resolves the story and is typically 25 per cent of the novel in length. The conflict should be resolved here and the character should have finished their journey. A climax should occur at the beginning of this act. Climaxes are sometimes associated with a big battle or fight, and it is where the conflicting forces collide.

So, to revisit our example: after our main character is rejected by his birth mother, he will meet her again and she will explain the reasons behind her behaviour towards him.

After the climax, we allow the reader to see how things have calmed down and how the conflict has been resolved. Our main character now understands why his mother gave him up, and meeting her has given him peace and allowed him to understand himself a lot better.

The vast majority of plays, films, and novels all follow this structure. Obviously, you do not need to stick rigorously to it but it can be a helpful way to see if your plot is working for you. Of course, not all novels follow this structure precisely, but if you start watching films or reading novels with this in the back of your mind you will begin to see how many exactly do follow this, and why exactly it works. You need to get into the habit of interrogating why films and other books work for you, and why the plot is interesting.

Write

I want you to look at the two earlier snapshot pieces you have done. You should have a one-sentence description of your book, and a one-page description of your book that gives more detail on character, setting, conflict and conclusion. From this, I want you to write a more extended synopsis that explains the plot of your book in detail – using the three-act structure. Ask yourself how the novel begins and what you need to use to begin the novel, write down what your inciting incident in the beginning will be. Then look at the middle and the action that will take place here, and the climax. Finally, focus on writing about what the ending will be. How will things conclude? How has the character been changed by their journey?

The inciting incident

The inciting incident and conflict are closely related to the *hook* of your novel. The hook is what gets people reading and gets them interested in your novel.

If *Harry Potter* was just about a boy at wizarding school, it is interesting but not *that* interesting – but throw in the hook that he killed the most dangerous wizard who ever lived but that wizard is back? Now there is a story worth reading.

Imagine that someone asks you 'Why would I want to read your novel?' how would you answer them? What are the main conflict and the inciting incident? In our earlier example story you might answer 'A boy discovers his parents aren't his real parents, but when he sets out to find his birth mother he quickly realizes that she has secrets of her own.'

Key idea

Figuring out the hook of your novel is a really good way to keep focused on the writing. In each chapter ask yourself 'is this furthering the plot, or developing character? If not, does it need to be here?'

I get a lot of submissions each month and my most common reason for stopping reading them is that the plot is not particularly well thought out: the conflict isn't well developed enough, or it is introduced too late. In some cases, the conflict seems to be completely non-existent. I then simply stop reading the work: readers would do the same. The best YA books keep you desperate to find out how things will resolve. The hook doesn't have to be hugely dramatic – such as Eragon fighting against the corrupt empire – but it does have to be intriguing and believable. For example, *The Last Summer of Us* by Maggie Harcourt (Usborne, 2015) is about the last summer three friends spend together on a road trip before they go their separate ways. A lot of secrets are revealed along the way and, even though the story is firmly grounded in relatable contemporary settings, it still has an intriguing hook and plot.

Sometimes opening lines can establish and hook the reader's interest. Work on developing a strong opening image or line, to get people reading. Working on a killer first line can also be really helpful when working on your novel outline in general.

Here are some examples:

- 'It has been sixty-four years since the president and the Consortium identified love as a disease, and forty-three since the scientists perfected a cure.'

    Delirium by Lauren Oliver (Hodder, 2011)

- 'Blue Sargent had forgotten how many times she'd been told that she would kill her true love.'

    The Raven Boys by Maggie Stiefvater (Scholastic, 2012)

- 'Newborn #485GA18M died on June 30, 2076, at 6:07 in the morning. She was three days old. The average lifespan of a human child, in the time since the break, was fifty-six hours.'

    Partials by Dan Wells (HarperCollins Children's Books, 2012)

- 'When the doorbell rings at three in the morning, it's never good news.'

    Stormbreaker by Anthony Horowitz (Walker, 2005)

- 'The first thing you find out when yer dog learns to talk is that dogs don't got nothing much to say.'

    The Knife of Never Letting Go by Patrick Ness (Walker, 2014)

All of these are immediately gripping and set the tone and voice for the rest of the novel. Most of them also introduce the hook or concept behind the novel right away, rather than taking a long time to develop the exposition needed to explain their settings and worlds.

Edit

Look back at the earlier 'write' exercise where you came up
with your more detailed synopsis. Ask yourself the following
questions:

- Does the plot feel big enough to sustain over 60,000 words?
- Do you have a strong cast of characters?
- Do you have subplots that act to complement and enhance
  your main plot?
- Is your conflict interesting and compelling?

Rewrite your synopsis based on your answers to these questions, to
ensure that it is a very strong planning document.

Conflict

Noun: A serious disagreement or argument, typically a protracted one

Verb: Be incompatible or at variance; clash

Stories revolve around conflict. Without conflict, a story can be
interesting, but it will ultimately be unsatisfying. If you were to
read a book about three little pigs who build three houses that they
live in, there is nothing really to draw the reader in. But throw in a
big bad wolf trying to blow their houses down, and their efforts to
overcome this, and immediately you have something far, far more
compelling. Novels without conflict are like a sandwich without
a filling – not particularly satisfying. One of my key reasons for
rejecting books is because of a lack of a story, or a lack of conflict.
You need something that drives the narrative along and keeps the
reader interested throughout on what is taking place, because they
know that there is a bigger issue at stake in the novel. Sometimes
this conflict can be a big, external force, or sometimes it can be an
internal conflict. Sometimes the most powerful novels do not feature
external conflicts, but are based around an internal issue that the
protagonist has to overcome.

You need to ask yourself, when you are planning a novel, 'Why is the reader reading this?' and 'What will the reader have discovered by the end of the novel?'

The basic types of conflict in fiction are traditionally 'man against man', 'man against nature', 'man against society' and 'man against self'.

Once you have decided on your conflict, you need to make sure that the conflict is:

- **believable** – would the conflict really happen? Will the reader believe in it?

- **not introduced too late** – you need to set up conflict from the very opening of the book in order to keep the reader reading; think hard about your inciting incident here.

- **appropriate for your audience** – would this conflict really apply to a YA audience? Make sure that this idea makes sense and that the conflict would feel believable and appropriate to them.

 Snapshot

If you have friends with teenagers, or have teenagers yourself, or know a teenager, run your conflict by them. Would the conflict affect them? Do they think it sounds true to life? If you do not know any teenagers, then go to your local library and chat to the YA librarian – see what they have to say.

A conflict can be big or small. Here are examples of two different types of conflict:

- *The Hunger Games* – the conflict here is huge! Katniss Everdeen has to kill 11 competitors in order to win her survival. She is also soon in conflict with the all-powerful Capitol, the rulers of her world.

- *The Duff* – the conflict here is much smaller. It is about a teenage girl who discovers that she is referred to as the 'designated ugly fat friend' and her conflict is about hiding the sexual relationship she has with a boy who bullies her, and dealing with her father's alcoholism.

Subplots and how to juggle them

It is important that you understand the central conflict of your novel, and the major plot that takes place. However, the majority of successful novels also feature smaller subplots. You do not need to get too hung up on how many subplots to have, or get carried away and have too many subplots distracting the reader. However, you should absolutely look at the other, smaller, plots taking place in the background of your novel.

Most subplots are used to complement and further the main plot. They typically involve things being made even more difficult for the protagonist! For example, the plot of your novel could be that your 16-year-old protagonist is investigating a mystery relating to disappearing classmates at her school. The subplots could be that her divorced father is trying to make contact with her, and she discovers that the boy she is in love with is secretly gay. Both of these will act to heighten the tension of the main plot, but not to overshadow it.

Often, each character in your novel represents a subplot. Your protagonist and antagonist are focused on the main plot, but what about the mean teacher, the bullying classmate, or the anxious best friend? They will have smaller plots of their own, which should always work alongside the main plot.

Write

I want you to write a piece about the main conflict in your novel, but weave into this the smaller conflicts we have just discussed. Use this exercise to explain what the conflict is and why it is important, but also explain how the smaller conflicts work their way into it too, to support or counterbalance the major conflict.

I want you to answer the following questions:

- How does your conflict take place?
- Who is affected by the conflict?
- How high are the stakes?
- Which characters are involved in the conflict?
- What is the climax of the conflict?
- How is the conflict resolved?
- How do the other conflicts work their way into the main conflict?
- Which of the subplot conflicts is most important?

How much to plot

Not everyone is a 100-per-cent pantser or a 100–per-cent plotter. Most writers find themselves to be a mixture of both. Once you have honed your one-sentence pitch, a more focused blurb, and considered the three-act structure and your conflict, you should be left with a really useful document which gives you insight into where your story is going and how you are going to get there.

However, some writers like to plan even further, and detailed planning can prove helpful, especially when you are writing your very first novel. Word counts can be flexible – as we've already discussed – but it can be helpful to keep in mind your goal word count as you begin to write. The three-act structure can also come into play here – if your novel is going to be 60,000 words long, then your first 15,000 words should be your first act, your next 30,000 words should be your second act, and the final 15,000 words should be your final act.

You can break this down even further as a guideline, however, and this can be a useful exercise to try out. One of my writers knows that each of his chapters is approximately 3,000 words long and knows how many chapters fall into each act. He also jots down one to five things that should take place in each chapter. These can be crucial, such as, 'in this chapter the battle takes place', or they can be small such as, 'include this conversation,' or 'character B needs to discover that character A has feelings for him.'

This means that, when he is planning, his plotting sheet looks like this:

ACT I

Chapter 1 (approx. 3,000 words)

Main character is introduced.

Worldbuilding - establishing parameters/rules of the world

Chapter 2 (3,000 words)

Main character discovers that his mother has been kidnapped

Main character meets antagonist

Dialogue between main character and sidekick which establishes what they can do to investigate

---

And so on.

While in some ways this level of detail might seem restrictive, it can also work as a safety net of sorts as the author always knows where they are going and what they need to achieve within each chapter. You can sometimes just write a single line or just one idea, which will give you an insight into how you need to shape the chapter and what will take place.

Beat sheets

Beat sheets are a common tool for screenwriting, but they can be just as helpful for plotting out a novel. In simple terms, a beat sheet is a collection of story beats – that is, a collection of scenes or elements of your story. Blake Snyder, in his book *Save the Cat!*, breaks down a simple beat sheet as the following 15 beats:

1 **Opening image:** establishes the tone/setting for the story

2 **Theme stated:** what will the story be about?

3 **Set-up:** things that need fixing

4 **The catalyst:** the life-changing event occurs

5 **Debate:** the character struggles with the idea of what they must do to deal with the catalyst

6 **Break into Act II:** the real story kicks in here, as the protagonist accepts their destiny

7 **B story begins:** normally this is the love story, but sometimes it can be a story of friendship, or another subplot

8 **Fun and games:** the kind of scenes you'd see in a trailer. The funny points and interesting moments.

9 **Midpoint:** point of clarity where the protagonist learns what they need

10 **The bad guys close in:** the obstacles get in their way – the protagonist's team unravels

11 **All is lost:** false defeat/no hope

12 **Dark night of the soul:** the protagonist has lost everything

13 **Break into Act III:** A story and B story combine and we find the solution to the catalyst

14 **The finale:** get rid of the bad guys and wrap it up

15 **Final image:** opposite of the opening image – focuses on what has changed[1]

I love Blake Snyder's beat sheet from *Save the Cat!* and, even though it is intended to be used for screenplays, I also think it can be incredibly helpful when plotting novels: I have at least two writers who use this when they come up with their story structure, and I always recommend it to my MA Creative Writing students.

---

[1] Blake Snyder, *Save the Cat!* (Michael Wiese Productions, 2005).

The best-laid plans of mice and men

One thing to bear in mind throughout is that plans can, and will change. Sometimes you might start out to write a novel about a boy who falls in love with his male next-door neighbour, but, before you know it, the book is about the next-door neighbour and his discovery of a drug-dealing ring at school. Do not be afraid of things like this happening to you during the creative process. It is a very normal part of proceedings. You are free to change your ideas at any time – things are not chiselled into stone!

One of my authors was 10,000 words into a new novel when she asked me for advice. She was setting the novel from two POVs in a historical setting, but as she hit 10,000 words she began to struggle with one of the voices. It didn't make historical sense for this voice to be there, and she had no logical way for the character to see what she needed her to see in order for the plot to progress. My advice was to scrap that POV character entirely and try the novel with just one POV, or to move it to an omniscient third-person voice instead.

The author was terrified, as she had planned the novel with these two POVs, but she agreed to give it a go. Two weeks later she had written 20,000 words in a fortnight. She had discovered that what had been shackling her word count was her insistence on sticking to the plan she had come up with. What she actually needed was flexibility even within this plan.

 Key idea

Keep suspense in mind when you are working on your novel. Consider the main questions your novel will ask, and if they will be answered by the end of the story. Some examples could be: will your main character ever find his birth mother? What secret is she hiding? Will he regret finding her? By the novel end, these should all have been answered in a satisfactory way.

Workshop

For the 'beat sheet' exercise, you used Blake Snyder's beat sheet as a way to develop a detailed breakdown of your novel, and to create an outline for it.

I want you to use this to answer the following questions:

- Is your logline interesting? Can your story be summed up in one sentence using our character, setting, conflict and conclusion format?
- Is your opening interesting? Does it grab the reader's attention?
- What are the big questions you are setting up to be answered?
- What is your A story? The A story is the main narrative arc of your novel.
- What is your B story?
- How do your A and B stories work together?
- How believable is your false ending? What does your hero lose?
- Is your middle section interesting and suspenseful?
- Is the story idea big enough to sustain an entire narrative?
- Are the obstacles your character has to overcome believable?
- Do you care about the main character?
- How much action takes place?

If there are any areas that need work, I want you to go back and look at them again, and revise your work. Once you have revised your work, answer the questions once more, until you can answer all of the questions in a satisfactory way.

In this chapter you have learned how to plot a novel. You have looked at hooks, conflicts and traditional story structure. You have completed a beat sheet. In the next stage we will be looking at characterization – how to develop a protagonist and an antagonist, and how to colour a cast of characters so that they feel believable and satisfying to your audience.

4

Characters

Now that we have looked at brainstorming and developing ideas, and planning, plotting and structuring your novel, it is time to look at developing your cast of characters. You can come up with the most interesting idea in the world, but if your characters are not interesting and believable, the story will ultimately fall flat. In this chapter we will look at developing your protagonist, antagonist and supporting characters. We will also look at how to flesh them out, key issues to avoid, and how to write pitch-perfect dialogue. By the end of this chapter you will have a much clearer idea of how to develop your bad guys as well as your good guys, how to ensure that your cast is believable to a young adult audience, and how to ensure that these characters are at the heart of your novel.

Ernest Hemingway

> *'When writing a novel a writer should create living people; people not characters. A character is a caricature.'*

Every novel has a protagonist – which means 'one who plays the first part, chief actor'. They are the main role in the novel, and typically they experience conflict because of the antagonist. When working out our plot for the novel, we talked about our key summary sentence: CHARACTER in SETTING experiences CONFLICT to CONCLUSION. This character we described is our protagonist, and the antagonist will most likely have some part to play within the conflict of the novel. Some books have more than one protagonist, and some books will focus on an antihero rather than a hero protagonist. However, most books, despite various supporting characters, have one clear protagonist. This does seem to be especially true in YA fiction.

For example, many book series make it very clear who the protagonist is. Thus, the Percy Jackson series, the Harry Potter series and the Alex Rider series all have their protagonist named in the series title.

You probably know from the start who your main character is going to be, and you should already know whether you will be writing them in the third person or the first person from the earlier chapter where we looked at different perspectives. Once you have decided who the protagonist is, it becomes important to understand as much as possible about them *before* you start writing. It is incredibly important to have an idea of your character's backstory, their motivation, how they look, what their personality traits are, any hidden secrets they may have, and how you plan for them to grow and change as the story progresses. It is very unsatisfying if a main character does not change or progress at all as the novel progresses: readers want to see the protagonist develop and change as they are affected by what happens to them during the course of the novel.

Characterization, and getting it right, is absolutely crucial when writing a novel. I see a lot of novels where the plot and setting are all good – but the characterization itself feels tacked on and half-hearted. These books are never a satisfying read.

Pitfalls to avoid

There are some very obvious pitfalls when it comes to writing characters, and you need to learn to identify and avoid these.

Often, I will see submissions where the character motivations do not make sense. It becomes clear that the author has made the character act a certain way to further the plot, when actually it seems very out of character for them to behave that way. You need to interrogate the choices you make for your characters, and make sure that if they act 'out of character' it is for a very clear reason, rather than just because you need them to do so to further the plot.

One of the most frustrating things for a reader is when characters perform in an unbelievable way. Sometimes, when reading a manuscript, I will say to the author: 'Why on earth did X confront Y?' and their answer will be 'Because they needed to for the sake of the plot.' No! That is never an acceptable answer.

Your characters should not be puppets, simply furthering the needs of a plot. They need to be realistic, living, breathing people who we can relate to. Have a real think about why a character acts a certain way at a certain time – maybe you need them to act this way for the sake of the plot, but you also therefore need to give them a believable and strong motivation for acting this way. It is always apparent to the reader when someone is doing something out of character, just because it helps along the plot.

A lot of writers pay attention to developing their good guys, but seem to do so at the expense of the rest of the cast. This can result in bad guys who feel like caricatures rather than people. We will look at how to ensure that you create scary, yet believable, villains later in this chapter, but it is something to be aware of from the start. This can also be true of the rest of your cast of characters. You might have a really great protagonist, with a lot of depth, but perhaps his three main friends all blur into the same person. You need to work to make sure that each character has a separate and distinct personality, and that the reader will be able to tell them apart.

You also need to be aware of the key facts about each of the characters, to ensure consistency in their age, name and background details. Often, crucial details about characters will change as the book goes on, as the author forgets what they have already written.

The list could go on: but the above illustrates that poorly written characters can really let your book down. You deserve to give your book the best possible chance in the world, so why skimp when preparing this crucial area? All of the above can be avoided by developing and keeping up to date a 'character bible' that you can easily refer to throughout the writing process.

 Key idea

You should plan your characters as much as you plan your novel. They are an integral part of the story and you need to give real thought to their growth and development.

Think like a journalist

When you are creating characters, you should try to think like an investigative journalist, out to sniff out a good story.

Start with the basics:

- name
- age
- birthday
- occupation
- address.

It is a sensible idea to write the answers to these questions down. Some authors use notecards and keep them in a file index; others prefer to use a document on their computer. The important thing is to keep these somewhere safe so that you can always refer to them easily when writing your book.

These first questions should be fairly simple and straightforward to fill in. You can change your mind as you go – but make sure that, if you do, you change these documents, and make the change everywhere in the text. There is nothing more confusing than reading a manuscript where Naomi suddenly becomes Rosie, or a 14-year-old character suddenly becomes 16.

Once you have the basics down, it is time to go a little deeper:

- favourite foods
- favourite films

- hobbies
- three favourite things
- three *least* favourite things
- favourite colour
- one thing they could not live without.

These answers are not one size fits all – maybe your character lives in a medieval world where there are no films – so be prepared to substitute other questions where appropriate for your text. But the idea is that you should be looking at the little personality quirks and interests that turn a character from 2D into 3D.

Looking at the character's background can really help when assessing their motivations and ensuring consistency across their characterization:

- family
- relationship with their family summed up in two sentences
- first kiss.

Understanding a character is absolutely crucial to writing them well, and believably. What they look like is less important, but even if the reader does not know what they look like, you should have an idea, as it might have an impact on how they carry themselves, or how people treat them.

I have read far too many novels where the character considers their reflection in front of the mirror at the very beginning, and I'm sure you have, too. It isn't necessary to give us an overly detailed depiction of how someone looks when you are writing a novel, but I do think that hints here and there will build up a picture of how someone looks – and sometimes these looks can be integral to the character. For example, in *Anne of Green Gables* it is Anne's red hair that leads her into many battles, including when Gilbert Blythe calls her 'carrots'.

It is important that you know how your character looks in your mind, but you can choose when to show those flashes of appearance through the text. Maybe someone at school bullies our heroine for having curly hair, or a 'big nose'. Maybe our heroine is self-conscious because she is going through puberty. Maybe our hero is so incredibly good-looking that girls are automatically drawn to him. Consider:

- height
- body type
- eye colour

- hair colour
- what they like to wear
- what they hate to wear
- one thing they would change about their appearance
- their favourite thing about their appearance.

The final question is a tricky one, but it's one that is crucial to know the answer to, in order to fully flesh out your character:

WHAT DO THEY WANT?

They could want something simple – like to be popular at school, or to kiss the boy of their dreams. Or it could be something more complicated – maybe they want their mum to stop hoping that their dad will come back home so that their family can move on. Maybe it is that they want the Empire of Kronifang to repel the False King. Maybe it is just that they want to have a warm bed to sleep in at night. Even your antagonists should want for something.

 ## Focus point

Understanding your characters will make them come alive. Do not skimp on fleshing them out, as even the information that you do not use on the page will still influence the decisions you make about your characters and how they act and react.

 ## Snapshot

Using the above bullet points, complete a profile of your main character. You can keep the answers brief, or expand on them where you feel it is appropriate, to build up a full understanding of who they are and what makes them tick. This will be the first entry in your 'character bible' – the first of many! Once you have perfected that, you should write two more character profiles: one for your antagonist and one for a supporting character. You need to get into the habit of paying as much attention to understanding your minor characters as you do to understanding your major ones. It can be hard to get under the skin of a villain, but you need to do so in order for them to be satisfying and believable to the reader.

Snapshot

Write a diary entry from the perspective of your protagonist, in first person, describing the funeral of a friend/family member. Focus on how they responded, who they spoke to, and most of all, how it made them feel. Were they sad? Did they feel guilty for not feeling more sad? Did they cry? Did they feel angry? Focus on showing these feelings as well as telling us about them.

Richard Bach

'If you will practice being fictional for a while, you will understand that fictional characters are sometimes more real than people with bodies and heartbeats.'

The best writers create characters that we understand. It does not mean we always approve of their actions, or that we would act the same way ourselves, but we should always at least understand their motivations. Knowing what each character wants is a very helpful way for the writer to approach creating a character. Even villains should want for something. Kurt Vonnegut says 'Every character should want something, even if it is only a glass of water.' This is completely true, and something you need to keep in mind when creating or developing characters.

Key idea

Know what your characters want, and make sure their motivations are always believable – and that they are not just doing things for the sake of the plot.

Chinua Achebe

'Once a novel gets going and I know it is viable, I don't then worry about plot or themes. These things will come in almost automatically because the characters are now pulling the story.'

Getting under the skin

Once you have developed these character sheets for your characters, writing should become easier. Obviously, these are just a jumping-off point, and you can change them in whatever way you feel necessary. Maybe you keep track of their friends, their hobbies, their favourite colour as well as everything else, but it really should be 'as well as' not 'instead of'. You need to get under the skin of these characters and stop them feeling like characters – they should feel like living, breathing people instead.

 Snapshot

> For this exercise I want you to write a job application from the perspective of your main character. You can take a fairly tongue-in-cheek approach to this – if it's a fantasy world maybe the job they would apply for is huntress, or general, or in a dystopian world perhaps they would be applying to be the lead defender of their camp of survivors. The important thing here is that you are writing from this character's perspective, in the first person. Talk about your key skills, mention your weaknesses, explain clearly why you would be an ideal applicant for the job. Focus on being as convincing as you can be – really get under the skin of your character and feel as if you are them.

There are a lot of exercises you can do to help you get under your character's skin. You can imagine how they would respond to various situations – and not necessarily those you are writing about in your book. You can picture them on their wedding day, or at a funeral, or during a job interview. Picturing your character in various scenarios and feeling confident about how they would act can be an incredibly useful exercise.

 Key idea

> The most satisfying characters are ones we can really empathize with and care about. If I don't care about your character, why do I want to find out what happens to them?

Salman Rushdie

'When I'm writing a book, sentence by sentence, I'm not thinking theoretically. I'm just trying to work out the story from inside the characters I've got.'

Show not tell

'Show, don't tell!' is one of those expressions writers hear a lot, but for very good reason. A lot of novels are hurt by their insistence on telling the reader things rather than letting us figure them out on our own. The reader is smart, and wants to be able to develop their own feelings about the characters without feeling as if the writer is telling us explicitly how we should feel about the characters. It is more satisfying to take a dislike to someone for our own reasons, rather than because the writer has told us that we should dislike that character.

Snapshot

Of the six examples below, three are telling us about a character's traits, and three are showing us what the character's traits are. Figure out which is doing which. How does it change your perception of the character when you come to your own conclusions rather than being told how to feel?

1 *He was a very nice guy, everyone at school thought so: he was friendly and kind to everyone he met.*

2 *'I'm very good at being cheerleading captain,' she said. 'I'm popular, athletic, and good at telling people what to do.'*

3 *The cat miaowed pitifully at his ankles. He looked around to see if anyone was watching and when he ascertained that he was alone, he violently kicked it away. 'Scat, go on, get out of here! I'm not your owner! Go and find him!'*

4 *She was a classic 'mean girl': unkind and spiteful, always with a witty one-liner but normally at someone else's expense.*

5 *He picked up the glass of orange juice from the table.*

> *'Hey, that's mine,' one of the year sevens exclaimed.*
>
> *'Correction,' he smirked, 'that was yours. Now? Now it is mine.'*
>
> *He downed the juice and smacked his lips exaggeratedly before leaning over and removing the rest of the boy's lunch.*
>
> 6 *The old woman was absolutely bedraggled. The rain had been coming down for a good five minutes and she was shivering. He ran over, his trousers slapping through the puddles. She shied away from him: he got that a lot, the scar on his face didn't exactly make him look pretty. But she persisted, 'Hey, here, have my umbrella.'*
>
> *She looked at him as if it might be a trick, but realized soon that it wasn't. 'Thank you,' she smiled, finally, sheltering under it.*

Instead of telling us that a character is good, show him doing something good – show him rescuing a stray dog, or giving money to a homeless man, or helping someone with their homework. Don't rely on saying 'she was nasty' but show us that she is an unkind person: show her picking on someone, making fun of someone's clothes, or laughing cruelly.

That isn't to say that it is wholly bad to 'tell'. Sometimes we need more detail about a scene, sometimes we need more information and exposition – but when it comes to characters it is always best to focus on the showing rather than just describing someone for us. There is more on this in Chapter 7.

Edit

Look at the six examples above. Examples 1, 2 and 4 are 'telling' us about the character. I want you to rework the above lines so they are 'showing' us rather than telling us.

- Rework 1 so we see that he is a nice, friendly and kind guy.
- Rework 2 so we see that she is popular, athletic and good at telling people what to do.
- Rework 4 so we can see her as unkind and spiteful.

Experiment with different ways to accomplish your goals.

Key idea

Know your character inside out. Even the information which isn't on the page isn't wasted, as knowing it will help you make decisions about your character which will shine through on the page.

Believable for the age range

We have already discussed making sure that your book is appropriate for a YA audience but this advice bears repeating, especially when considering character. We have talked about how your protagonist should be a little older than your target market, but you also need to make sure that your protagonist actually acts as if they are this age. Read up on popular bands, popular clothes, popular slang; become aware of what they would be studying at school, and how emotionally intelligent they would be. Nothing dates a book more than bands which are out of favour being listened to by teen characters – so maybe consider making up your own.

You also need to make sure that you dress your character in a believable way. If your character is a 14-year-old boy he will probably wear baggy jumpers, baggy jeans and trainers. Dressing him in chinos and deck-shoes might be how you want your 14-year-old to dress, but it won't make him feel believable! Look at what teenagers are wearing and where they are shopping, too.

Make sure that your character's wants and needs are in keeping with those of other children/teenagers their age. Reading teen magazines can be a really useful way of seeing what preoccupations a teenage audience has – although you will probably find that they are not too dissimilar from your own preoccupations when you were a teenager!

Look also at the vocabulary you have your characters using. Some teenagers do talk using a complex vocabulary full of adult words, but most do not. That is not to say that you need to make sure that your characters talk in a very simplistic way – do *not* patronize a teen audience! – but you do need to make sure that they sound the way teens actually talk. As well as clothes, slang expressions can really date a book. If your characters are saying 'golly' or 'gosh' in a modern-day world, it feels unbelievable. Do not rely too much on slang: use it now and then, but only in the way an actual teenager would, not relying on it to prop up the text. One thing that pulls me out of a novel very fast is too much slang. This seems to be especially apparent in futuristic worlds where the author has created their own slang: they use it far, far too heavily. Think of slang words as like seasoning: you do not want too many of them and they should be enhancing the flavour of the book rather than masking it. As Hemingway said: 'Try and write straight English; never using slang except in dialogue and then only when unavoidable ... slang goes sour in a short time.'

Even in a dystopian world or a science-fiction universe, your teenagers should still feel like teenagers. Maybe they dress differently, or have bigger issues to deal with, but at their heart they should still feel relatable for your teenage market. Look at Katniss in *The Hunger Games*: yes, she is saving the world, but she also worries about her family and the boy she loves. Or Harry Potter: he cares about crushes and bullies as well as caring about how he is to go about defeating Lord Voldemort. No matter how fantastical the world you have created is, it still needs to have familiar touchstones for your readership.

 Focus point

Make sure that your characters read as believable for the age range you are aiming the book at. It is important to make sure that their concerns – and how they look, act and dress – feel accurate for their age.

Bad guys and flawed heroes

 Terry Pratchett

'For an author, the nice characters aren't much fun. What you want are the screwed-up characters. You know, the characters that are constantly wondering if what they are doing is the right thing, characters that are not only screwed up but are self-tapping screws. They're doing it for themselves.'

A common flaw, especially in YA novels where writers are often trying to impart a moral lesson, is creating cookie-cutter bad guys, or heroes who are too perfect, which we touched upon earlier in this chapter.

You absolutely need to have a protagonist who people root for, and you need to make sure that your reader is invested in their character journey. But that is absolutely not the same thing as creating a protagonist who seems completely perfect. It is not interesting to read about a beautiful, straight-A student who gives to charity, helps the homeless, is brilliant at sport and has a perfect love life. Every character should have a flaw. Give me a beautiful, straight-A, kind student with a perfect love life who is secretly battling bulimia and immediately you make me more interested in them. These 'imperfections' can help bring a character to life on the page.

There has been a real run of heroines with unrealistic 'flaws' lately. The character is perfect, but she has mismatched eyes, or the character is perfect except for being clumsy. But these flaws aren't really flaws at all; instead, they feel like a lazy shorthand for making someone feel more likeable. Start paying attention to people you know, characters in films, or public figures. Try to identify what their weakness is, as well as their strength. It could be that they have a stutter. It could be that they suffer from severe stage fright. It could be that they are loyal, to a fault, to a friend who is not looking out for them. It could be a physical thing but it could just as easily be a mental thing: maybe they are chronically shy, or suffer from night terrors, or lose their temper too easily. These things will not make the reader shy away from liking them; it will just make them feel a lot more real to your audience.

It is also very important to work hard on your antagonist. Your snapshot exercise on writing character profiles should have helped you develop your antagonist in a more well-rounded way, and start to understand them more, but it is a lesson which bears repeating. I am not saying that every villain needs to be secretly suffering from an illness, or have had a horrible childhood, but we need to have some sort of sense of why they act in the way that they do.

Focus point

In real life, no one is wholly bad or wholly good. People are shades of grey. Sometimes good people make bad choices, and sometimes bad people can surprise you, too. Do not make your characters too black or too white, as we need to have a sense of those shades of grey.

Let us remember also that characters can grow through a narrative: in fact, they absolutely should develop and change over the course of the novel. That isn't to say that, by the end, your villain should be a hero, but your villain should certainly have learned a little something along the way. A good example of a character who grows and changes over the course of a story is Cordelia in the TV series *Buffy the Vampire Slayer*. At the start of the series, Cordelia is spoiled, cruel, shallow and selfish. By the end of the series Cordelia has experienced a lot of supernatural danger and had to put herself in harm's way for the sake of others. In the process she has learned a lot more about herself. She can still act spoiled and shallow, but she is a lot more selfless than when the story started out, and she is a stronger and more likable character for it.

Similarly, Draco Malfoy in the Harry Potter series reveals himself as not as evil as Harry had suspected. Draco is torn by loyalty to his family and not wanting to do the Dark Lord's bidding. He has come a long way from the spoilt brat of the first book, to someone whom Harry Potter can reluctantly respect, if not like.

Dialogue

Dialogue can be very hard for the author to get right, but if it does work, it can lend shade and tone to the novel very successfully. Dialogue can add depth to characters; it can further the plot; it can push the story forward. In the right hands, it is a brilliant tool! On the flipside, few things make me want to put a book down more than bad dialogue.

There are several key tips to bear in mind when writing dialogue:

1 **Start to listen to how other people talk.** Go to a coffee shop with a notebook and pay attention to the conversations that take place

around you. What slang do people use? What are the natural rhythms of their speech? Where do they abbreviate words? Where do they get their expressions from? By listening to how people talk, you can start to learn how to set that down on the page in a believable way.

2 **Do not rely too heavily on exposition.** A key mistake writers make is to put facts or backstory into the conversation, in a way that just does not seem natural at all. You should never write 'as you know…' because it seems false. 'As you know, your father left seven years ago.' 'As you know, you have a small brown dog.' If someone already knows something, why would the speaker be telling them it? There are ways to share information so it seems natural – perhaps your dialogue takes place in a classroom, or between a tutor and a pupil. But in general, avoid feeding the reader too many important facts through dialogue.

3 **Watch out for using someone's name too many times!** This is a common issue I see in dialogue, John. People rely too much, John, on saying the person's name. But real conversations do not go like that, John. Look through your own writing, and spot whether you are peppering the dialogue with names. If so, strike them out, as using names slows things down and stops the dialogue feeling natural.

4 **Make sure that your dialogue is all killer and no filler.** Edit out the boring bits. If someone perfectly transcribed a conversation it would be full of *you know*s, *ers* and *ums*, which is not very interesting to read. Ask yourself whether your dialogue is furthering the plot or furthering character: if it is doing neither of those things, does it really need to be there at all?

5 **Remember not to make speech too formal,** unless the character is very formal. Very few people speak the Queen's English perfectly. Rather than 'I do not recollect what you mean', a teenager would be more likely to say 'I don't remember'. Most people use contractions when they speak (*isn't, didn't, won't, don't*), so to get rid of all of these unless it is in keeping with your character makes the dialogue feel jarring on the ear.

6 **Try not to rely too much on dialogue.** A page of unbroken exposition will feel boring for the reader, but so, too, will a page of unbroken dialogue. Try to intersperse the dialogue with

actions, where appropriate. Sometimes an action can speak louder than words. Maybe when your character has been asked a difficult question he starts to gnaw on a hangnail, or fidgets in his chair and looks away. Perhaps he gets up, or starts doodling on a pad. All of these actions tell us as much as what the character is saying, so use these moments where appropriate too, to add colour and depth to the writing.

Key idea

You need enough dialogue to bring the text to life, but too much and you can end up distracting from and slowing down the plot of the novel. Do not over-rely on dialogue: you need to make sure that it serves a purpose and is not just there to take up space.

Write

Write a page of dialogue between your protagonist and antagonist. Then take away the indicators of who is talking. Read the dialogue aloud: can you tell which sentences belong to each character? How? They should have different ways of speaking, using different turns of phrase and different idioms. The reader should be able to tell you who is speaking just from how they speak, the phrases they use and what they are saying.

Voice

Voice can be one of the hardest things to get right. The fact that agents and editors put so much store by 'voice' is probably intensely annoying for writers because there seems to be no single definition of what 'voice' really means. I am guilty of saying 'I love a fresh voice' or 'I want a gripping voice'. But what is 'voice' and how do you get one?

Don Fry, in *Writing Tools: 50 Essential Strategies for Every Writer*, uses this definition: 'Voice is the sum of all the strategies used by the author to create the illusion that the writer is speaking directly to the reader from the page.'

Whenever I am asked about 'voice' and what it means, I like to direct people to some of the strongest voices I have read in fiction:

- *Vernon God Little* by D.B.C. Pierre
- *I Capture the Castle* by Dodie Smith
- *The Crimson Petal and the White* by Michel Faber
- *The Knife of Never Letting Go* by Patrick Ness

All of these novels have a very distinct 'voice' that sets them apart from books by other writers. They are also possibly 'Marmite' books – you either love them or you hate them! But they definitely provoke a reaction.

A simple way to think about voice is to see it as style. What style does the author use? What style do you use? Why do you connect more with this piece of writing than that piece of writing?

Examining the following can help you get under the skin of authorial voice:

- **Dialogue vs description** How much dialogue do you use? Are there a lot of descriptive passages or is the bulk of the novel told using dialogue? Is the dialogue naturalistic or dramatic?
- **Metaphor and simile** How often do you use metaphors and similes in the text, and similar descriptive tricks? Do you spell a lot of things out or leave them to the imagination?
- **Sentence length** Some sentences can be short. Punchy. Aggressive. Other sentences can be long, and flowing, utilizing commas and dashes and being expansive. Which do you prefer?
- **Point of view and tense** Do you use first or third person? How close is the POV? Is the novel all told in an immediate present tense? Or is it told in the past tense?

Obviously, voice is more than just these things, but these factors can certainly change a voice or help bring it to life. There are some writers whose voice you can pick up no matter what they are writing. Others prefer to fade into the background, letting their characters do the talking for them.

Write

Through this chapter you will have picked up various tips and tricks about how to develop characters, and how to make them believable. Now we are going to use those tips and tricks for a writing exercise. I want you to write two diary entries. The first diary entry will be from your protagonist's point of view, detailing their first encounter with the antagonist of the novel. The second will be from the antagonist's point of view, detailing their first encounter with the protagonist of the novel. Focus on getting across their different motivations, their different perspectives, their ways of speaking and writing.

Workshop

Look back at your previous 'write' exercise and consider the following:

- Are the voices distinct?
- What makes the voices different from one another?
- Whose account is the most convincing?
- Is the language used believable for the age range?
- Are their concerns realistic for the age range you are writing for?
- Can you tell the character's motivations from the piece?
- Do you over-rely on dialogue?
- Is there too much description?
- Which piece is the more interesting to read?
- Why is that piece more interesting than the other?

Now, look over your answers. Rewrite each piece, bearing in mind your answers to the questions. Now go through the pieces again to check that you have answered the questions. Your ultimate aim is to make both accounts as convincing and as interesting as each other – considering character motivation and development through the writing.

Next step

In this chapter you have learned how to create characters, how to make them believable, how to describe their motivation, and how to develop author voice and dialogue. In the next chapter we are going to look at worldbuilding. You have successfully created interesting characters – now you need to create a world that is as interesting as they are!

5

Worldbuilding and describing your world

In the last chapter we looked at characterization: how to create characters, what you needed to know about them, and how to make this come across on the page. In this chapter we are going to look at 'worldbuilding' (a term now so pervasive in creative writing that it is written without the expected hyphen): how to develop a setting, how to make it believable, and how to describe your world in ways that add to the tone and interest of your novel.

Worldbuilding literally refers to building a fictional world or universe. This can mean that you are creating a wholly new world (normally referred to as a 'secondary world') or it can refer simply to fleshing out the world which your characters inhabit, and making that seem real and believable to your readers.

Worldbuilding is a lot more complicated than just your 'setting' and the geography of the world – although that comes into it, too. Worldbuilding is about anything and everything that takes place within that world: what it looks like, what the currency is, the life expectancy, religion, sex, culture, clothing and everything in between.

I imagine some of you are sitting there thinking, 'Yeah, I guess that's important if you are writing a complicated fantasy or science-fiction novel! But what about my contemporary romance?'

Worldbuilding is just as important in contemporary fiction as it is in more fantastical fiction. Maybe you do not have to consider as many complicated things if you set your novel in a small town in the UK but you will need to consider a lot of the concerns mentioned above when building anything more complicated. Whatever the world of your novel, you will still need to consider what matters to the characters, what their goals are, how much money they have, what their life trajectories are going to be, and everything in between. You need to work to create an interesting and believable world – and also one that makes sense to your readership. Maybe that makes it easier to set your book on Mars, or maybe it makes it more difficult.

In some novels, the world is just as important as the characters, and descriptions of the setting can become as much a part of the novel to enjoy as the rest of the writing.

For example, Harry Potter's Hogwarts takes on a life of its own. And there are few people who have read *The Lord of the Rings* who aren't fascinated by the world of Middle Earth. These writers put in a lot of care and attention into creating interesting settings. But even if your setting is someone's home, their school and their friend's houses, you can still work to make it fully fleshed out and serve more purpose than just a bland backdrop.

Describing your world falls under worldbuilding – and once you have all the aspects worked out in your head, how do you convey them to the reader in a way which doesn't feel heavy-handed, or slow the story down? Some writers overwrite and give us way too much information and a lot of description, which results in slowing the story down. We should experience the world as the character does: this is a novel, after all, not a travelogue or a reference book. Other people underwrite. They do not give us enough information or detail, which can result in a book feeling confusing. Often, when I finish reading an underwritten novel, I will have a lot of questions for the author about the setting. Often, the author knows the answers but they just haven't come through clearly enough in the writing. In this chapter we will look at ways to make sure that you get the balance right, ensuring that your description is an interesting and complementary part of your writing experience.

Iain M. Banks

'The trouble with writing fiction is that it has to make sense, whereas real life doesn't.'

People tend to fall into three different categories when it comes to worldbuilding:

1 Those who just write, without any worldbuilding preparation, and hope it falls into place as they go along.

2 Those who know the rough rules for their world and plan to figure the rest out as they go along.

3 Those who write a 'world bible' before they start, addressing any issues which take place in the world, even before they begin.

As with so much writing advice, there is no one 'correct' way to do it. Some massively bestselling writers do little to no worldbuilding preparation. Others do huge amounts. More fall somewhere in between. But when you are just starting out, I think it is for the best to be absolutely prepared when it comes to writing your novel. It is best to sit down and properly plan it out, rather than diving head first into a world and then surfacing a few chapters in and realizing that things don't make any sense, and that you have to go right back to square one. This is much the same approach as I have encouraged you to take with your plot and characters, simply applied to your world as well.

A lot of writers start off with a rough idea and then keep going, but you can very easily write yourself into a corner that way. You might end up 10,000 words in before you realize that the characters could not do this in the world you have created, or that suddenly you need to rewrite the opening in order to compensate for a setting change. You need to consider some big questions in your novel before you can start writing it. Preparation is the key to success!

Key idea

Rushing into a novel without considering your world is a sure-fire way to find yourself skidding to an abrupt halt partway through the text. Research and plan and you will find yourself better equipped to finish an entire novel rather than having to stop a little way into it.

Think of two of your favourite YA novels. Write a paragraph for each, explaining the world in which they are set, which could be used by someone who has never read them as an introduction into these worlds. An example could be explaining the Districts that are involved in *The Hunger Games*, or describing the time period and geographical setting of *Eleanor & Park*. Whether fantasy or non-fantasy, worldbuilding plays a role in every novel.

Notes and background

Before you begin a novel, I think it is very important to have at least figured out the basics of the world that you have created. You have to spend 50,000 to 100,000 words in this world – you need to know how it works!

Research is the backbone of worldbuilding. Even if your novel is set in a fantasy or science-fiction world, it should still have enough familiarity for it to make sense to readers. There are a lot of resources out there to help you when you are planning your novel. You can find help online, or through reference books at your local library. Maybe you don't know how many GCSEs most teenagers take in the UK off the top of your head, but the information is out there if you deliberately look for it.

Wattpad is a website where people can upload their novels as they go along, where readers can comment on them as they are uploaded. There have been several famous YA writers to come out of the site, such as Beth Reekles (*The Kissing Booth*) and Abigail Gibbs. One issue with a website where you are uploading as you write is that you cannot go back and fix earlier problems with the text. Many authors will be uploading a chapter a day, or a chapter a week, and be writing constantly to get their content ready in time. Often, major flaws in the worldbuilding become apparent when you are partway through the story, but it is too late by then to fix them. This shows how important it is to plan your world before you begin writing – then you can avoid these issues or confront them up front, rather than trying to deal with them during the writing process.

HISTORICAL FICTION

If your book is set in the past, it is an absolute must for you to do your research. That is not to say that you need to find yourself handcuffed to the facts: this is a novel, so of course it is OK to experiment and have fun, but if it is purporting to be historically accurate then you need to make sure that it is historically accurate. What did people wear? How did they eat? What slang did they use? What was the political system? What was their religious system? What were their surroundings like?

Poor historicism can immediately switch me off from a book. It can become quickly apparent that the author does not know very much about the time period, which means that I stop caring very quickly.

There is nothing more jarring than reading a historical novel and seeing really modern things, maybe something that had not been invented yet or a really modern term. Those can quickly pull the reader from the narrative, and make them aware of its artifice. It also feels very lazy because if you are committing to write a book in a world, you should also commit to doing the necessary research before you start writing it.

There is a wealth of information online but – and I cannot emphasize this enough – always check your sources. You don't want to rely on something that you later discover to be completely inaccurate. Your local library will have a lot of reference books and biographies you can check out, and, if possible, try visiting some of the sites you are writing about.

FANTASY NOVELS

Most fantasy novels have some basis in our 'primary world', whether it is pseudo-medieval or steampunk. You need to do a lot of research into the era you are inspired by, into weaponry and warfare, and clothing and geography. Of course, this is a novel, so you can change things (dragons!) and get rid of things (famine!) as you so choose, but you do need to still have enough research behind it to support your world.

Even fantasy novels which are set in our world, but with fantastic elements, need a focus on worldbuilding and rules. For example, in *Half Bad* by Sally Green, the witches live alongside humans but they are mostly unaware of each other. Sally Green needed to work to explain how they lived so separately, and what happened when their worlds collided and people were hurt. Knowing the limitations of your world is very important to establishing the story in a satisfying way.

SCIENCE-FICTION NOVELS

Keep it consistent, and keep it logical. If your futuristic world runs on energy that comes from goat's milk, have some sort of logical explanation behind this. If your novel is set in space, consider the impact of gravity, of loneliness, or what the atmosphere does to the human body if you are sucked out into it. What is their economy like? Why? What is the weather like? Why? Are there androids? Do they have human rights, too? Consider these things before you start writing, not partway through the text when you are stuck in a corner and wondering how to get out.

CONTEMPORARY NOVELS

Maybe your novel is set in Milton Keynes, and you live in Milton Keynes, so you do not think you have to research it. However, some of the details that are familiar to you will not be familiar to your readers. Some of the details that seem interesting to you will not be interesting to your readers. Research is the backbone of all good novels. Most teen novels are going to have a school setting, so research the school setting. Do they wear uniform? Is it a private school or a state school? How old are they when they sit their GCSEs? Are they legally allowed to work at a pizza parlour at their age? How old is too old to be admitted to dance school?

EVERYTHING IN BETWEEN

In case I have not made myself clear yet – research your setting. Research every aspect of it. Maybe these facts won't make it into the finished text, but you should still know them in the back of your mind.

Snapshot

Write a short piece describing the main setting of your novel, to give to tourists when they arrive. This place can be someone's house, it can be a castle, or it can be a spaceship, whichever is appropriate to your novel. Cover the key points that anyone visiting this place would need to know. Are there fierce dogs? Is there acid rain? Is there a really awful bully that lives there, too? Keep it brief and snappy, and just give them the ten key bullet points about the main setting.

Mapping it out

A lot of fantasy novels contain maps, and it can be a really handy guide for you if you draw one when you begin your novel. How long does it take your character to walk from the city of Glenorble to their home of Whizzbang? Can they go by horse and carriage? Would they be able to drive there?

In contemporary novels, too, you need to consider lots of factors. How big is your town? How cosmopolitan is it? How many people live there? Is there an airport? A bus station? A train station? These factors can certainly affect how believable your novel feels to the reader. For example, if your novel is about a boy who yearns to become an actor and escape his humdrum town, if you set it in London it starts to feel unbelievable. However, if you set it in a tiny village in the Scilly Isles, the central conflict starts to make a lot more sense to the reader.

What is the weather like? Is the sky a uniform grey, or is it absolutely burning hot like the Sahara? Does it rain regularly? Sometimes the weather can become just as much of a feature of mood as the characters' own mood. *Twilight* feels moodier because it is grey and cloudy all year round. Hogwarts feels scarier because of the extremes of weather that take place there. These factors can add colour and shape to your novel.

Is the sky grey, purple or somewhere in between? Is the school mostly concrete, or with dreamy spires and majestic towers? Is the protagonist's home in a grey and uniform block, or a cramped bedsit, or a colourful cottage?

If you can get to the place where your novel is set, then try to visit it for research and for fact-checking. It's a novel, not a travel guide, so no one expects 100-per-cent accuracy, but some mistakes are easily avoided. A friend – and YA author – visited central London for the first time and quickly realized that her epic fight scene would need a different setting because the two buildings she mentioned were miles apart.

 Snapshot

Draw a map based on your setting, highlighting any key points of interest. If this was Harry Potter's world, you might highlight Hogwarts, the Ministry of Magic, the Weasleys' house and the Dursleys' house. If it was set in a contemporary world, you might highlight the local school, the club the kids hang out in and the park. Think about which settings are most important to your text and illustrate these.

 Focus point

Creating a whole world can feel overwhelming, so try to focus on small factors first of all. Where does your main character spend most of their time? What does this look like? Which other main places do they visit? What are these places like for them? If you stare at a blank page as if you are about to write an entire essay about a world, it can certainly feel overwhelming, but if you focus on the main settings and work from there it suddenly becomes a much more manageable task.

 Stephen King

'Description is what makes the reader a sensory participant in the story. Good description is a learned skill, one of the prime reasons you cannot succeed unless you read a lot and write a lot. It's not just a question of how-to, you see; it's a question of how much to. Reading will help you answer how much, and only reams of writing will help you with the how. You can learn only by doing.'

Everyone needs rules

So your world has a series of giant demons who can suck people's brains out. OK, but we still need rules for the demons: whose brains can they suck out? How can they be defeated? Where do they come from? Superman is an unstoppable force but his weakness is kryptonite and this stays consistent throughout the comics, the TV series and the films. If that was suddenly changed, and the creators 'broke the rules', the world would stop making sense.

In a contemporary world we still need rules. What gets a character suspended? What makes them get punished with detention? When will their parents get angry with them? We need consistency throughout or the reader starts to lose patience with the world.

In the section on structure, we looked at inciting incidents: the moments that kick the story up a gear. A key thing to bear in mind with these is to make sure that they make sense within the context of your world. For example, if the novel starts off with famine encroaching, make sure that you are aware of why famine is encroaching now and not, say, 20 years earlier. The background to the inciting incident feeling plausible is a key factor in the success of a novel. Make sure that you figure out why now, and that it makes sense in the context of your world.

You also need to work hard to set your stakes for the novel. Stakes can differ depending on the world. For example, for Harry Potter in the early books, the stakes are that he does not want to be expelled from school and forced to live with his hated aunt and uncle. In the later books, the stakes are that he doesn't want his world destroyed at the hands of Lord Voldemort. Maybe your stakes are that your character needs to kiss someone or they lose a bet, or that they need to discover who their real father is otherwise they will be forced into care. Or maybe your stakes are that the world is about to end and your character is the only one who can stop this. Make sure that the stakes make sense for the world you have created, and that they seem believable and appropriate.

Focus point

No matter what your world is like, it needs to make sense for a young adult audience, and it needs to feel accessible and believable for your target market. The ways that teens look at things are different from how adults look at things. Some things that matter deeply to adults do not matter to a young adult audience, and vice versa. Make sure that your setting feels realistic for your characters, and for your intended readership.

Key idea

Not everything that is in your research document will make it into your novel. That is normal, and a positive thing, as you do not want to overcrowd and slow the text down. But it is very important that you understand as much about your world as possible, and then filter on to the page what is important for us to have an understanding of, too.

Describing your world

OK, so you've researched your world and you know the basics of it. Now consider what it looks like and how best to describe it to the reader so that it comes alive for them, too. You should be aware, though, that too much description can really make a reader switch off. You need to strike a balance between giving us enough of interest to whet our appetite, and having us feel overwhelmed with information. You never want to have vast swathes of description, as the reader will just end up skimming them, and might miss some important details in the sea of adjectives.

Consider this paragraph as an example of overusing description:

He opened the purple front door and walked into the grey hallway. On his right was a big-framed picture of Kara's family. Her mum had red hair, like Kara, and her brothers' hair was dark brown. Her dad looked sternly out of the photograph, while Kara looked dreamily away. She was so beautiful, but never seemed to realize it. Ahead of him was the blue door, which led into the kitchen. He opened the door, noticing how it creaked, which made him jump. The kitchen was empty, apart from Kara's cat, who was fat and tortoiseshell, with a red collar on. The kitchen had high ceilings, and was very clean – it smelled strongly of bleach. He wrinkled his nose and walked towards the fridge, opening the tall silver unit and pulling out a can of coke. He closed the door and walked towards the pine table, pulling out a stool and rearranging the green cushion on it. The cat miaowed angrily at him, until he reached out and scratched him behind the ears. Kara should have been home by now. He looked up towards the tall grandfather clock to confirm his suspicions. Yes, she was twenty minutes late. She knew how uncomfortable the pristine nature of her house made him, and he was annoyed that she had left him alone in their mansion. He knew her parents saw him as 'Bob, the caretaker's son,' and would never see him as more than that no matter what he did, no matter how long he dated their daughter. He sighed and shifted on the chair, flicking through the newspaper that was folded on the counter as he waited.

What important information do we get from this about the character or the setting? All we know is that Kara and Bob are a couple, that her family are rich, and that they look down on Bob because his family are not rich. The rest of the description is boring and unnecessary.

Edit

Have a go at rewriting the above paragraph, in a way which gets across the same information but in a much more interesting way. Rather than focusing on the exact specifications and layout of where Bob is walking, focus on his feelings and on description that adds something to our understanding of the text. You can be really creative here, and add your own interpretation to the characters and setting.

Using your senses

When we write, we almost always focus on how things look. But how about the other senses? Focusing on the other senses can make the writing process more interesting – and it can definitely help bring a scene or setting to life for your reader.

HEARING

What we hear can have a huge impact on our feelings or experience of a place. Think about how sound is used in horror films, for example – lack of sound can be just as effective as loud and sudden noises. Think about what your character might hear as he or she enters a place. When walking into school, will she be overwhelmed by loud teenagers, and by teachers yelling, and the school bell ringing? Waiting for his first kiss, might he be conscious of his heart beating loudly in his ears? As he walks through the graveyard, might he be aware of how silent it is, and how his heart jumps as he hears a twig suddenly crack? Sounds can be an incredibly useful tool for adding mood to a setting.

TASTE

Obviously, it would be weird if your main character walked around licking everything! But there is a time and a place for when taste can really add to the mood and setting of a piece. Perhaps they are eating the first meal that they have had all day; think of how Charlie in *Charlie and the Chocolate Factory* tastes chocolate:

> 'Charlie grabbed it and quickly tore off the wrapper and took an enormous bite. Then he took another ... and another ... and oh, the joy of being able to cram large pieces of something sweet and solid into one's mouth! The sheer blissful joy of being able to fill one's mouth with rich solid food!'

Some of the best writers can make us hungry, just by their descriptions of the taste of something.

SMELL

You probably do not notice it much, but everything around you has a smell. There are obvious ones like the smell of manure that lingers in your nostrils, or a strong smell of aftershave. But try closing your eyes for a minute and thinking about what you can smell. Is it wet dog? Is it freshly mown grass, or maybe just washing powder? Think about how what you can smell adds to the mood of a place. It can make something feel comforting, or frightening.

TOUCH

How does something feel when you touch it? Think about the difference between holding hands with someone when their hands are sweaty, and holding hands with someone when their hands are dry and warm. What does it feel like to stroke a dog? How does it feel when you climb inside freshly laundered sheets, or when you slip in the mud?

SIGHT

This is what most writers focus on when describing a scene. Of course, it is a very important factor in describing a setting, but it is important to remember that it is not by any means the only way to describe a setting.

Write

Pick a room or setting that is important to your protagonist. This could be their bedroom, or somewhere broader like their school. Describe the room, working through all of the senses. What can your character hear? Does the air taste of anything – like salt if they are near the sea? What can they smell? What do the objects in the room feel like to touch? Finally, how does it look? Try to spend at least two pages describing the room from the perspective of each of the five senses.

Getting to the point

It is a real skill to describe a world or setting without using too many words. In the previous 'edit' exercise we looked at cutting back on useless information and focusing on getting to the point. A common error writers make is using too many adverbs to describe a place.

Contrast this:

> The room was very dark, with heavy curtains and thick oriental rugs. Every surface was crammed with ornaments in every colour under the sun, and it had a thick and cloying smell of perfume that caught in the back of her throat. Even though it was sunny outside her grandmother had the curtains drawn and the floral wallpaper made the room feel small and oppressive.

with this:

> The room was cluttered and her grandmother kept the curtains drawn, making the room feel oppressive.

Both convey a similar feeling to the room, but the second does so in a much more succinct way.

 ## Focus point

Reading poetry and short stories can be a really good way to learn how to sketch your setting in very few words.

The iceberg theory

Otherwise known as 'the theory of omission', this was the minimalistic writing style employed by Ernest Hemingway. Hemingway believed that truth in a story often lurked beneath the surface – that the real meaning of a story never needed to be explicitly discussed but could instead be gleaned from the surface-level detail. Most of the knowledge you have about your characters and world will not make it into your story, but this knowledge will influence the story that your readers see.

You only ever see 10 per cent of an iceberg – the remaining 90 per cent is always below the surface. The same should be true of your worldbuilding. Only 10 per cent of what you know about the world should ever be present on the page – but the remaining 90 per cent is what holds the rest of the iceberg up, giving it shape and support.

You should work to include this worldbuilding in a seamless way. Pages and pages of exposition are boring for the reader, and slow the story down. Look at finding ways to share the information with subtlety so not too much of it is shown on the page, but so that the reader can trust that you know where the story is going.

Write

Imagine that you are dropped slap bang into the middle of the world of your novel. Write a letter to a friend or family member, explaining where you are, and what life is like. Pay attention to your geographical surroundings, the people, the mood of the place, and how you spend your days. Try to make sure that this reads like an interesting and informative letter, rather than a list. Focus on feelings and mood, as well as on empirical facts about the world surrounding you.

Chuck Wendig, *25 Things You Should Know about Worldbuilding*

'*What's true for other stories is true with a story featuring thick, delicious worldbuilding – you're better off conveying the details of that world through action and dialogue than through giant boulders of description and exposition dropped on your readers from a vertiginous height.*'

Exposition dumps

One of the biggest turn-offs for a reader is big, heavy paragraphs full of description and background information. These are known as 'exposition dumps'.

Exposition is defined as 'writing or speech primarily intended to convey information or to explain; a detailed statement or explanation; explanatory treatise'.

It can be very jarring to come across heavy exposition in a novel. It is much better to slowly reveal information in clever ways. Rather than having a character describe their own appearance as they look in the mirror, perhaps their messy hair comes up in conversation when their mother tells them to brush it. Or rather than having a character describe their bedroom, we see more of it when their little brother is caught nosying around the room and they fight over where he found her diary. Having the characters interacting with their surroundings, and with the setting of the novel, can be a really interesting way to give us the information we need without it feeling heavy-handed.

A key issue with exposition can be that what the writer finds interesting actually has no place in the story. Perhaps in your world there are aliens that crash-landed and only communicate through interpretative dance. But if they add nothing to the story, or characters, then why do they need to be there?

I remember one author who had a throwaway paragraph mentioning an alien invasion. It had no relevance to the story and was quite distracting. I asked her why it was there. 'I just thought it was cool,' she said. This can be a common pitfall. You are inventing tons of things about your world and you will have all of this information about it that you are desperate to share – but that doesn't mean it needs to be shared. Remember the iceberg theory – 90 per cent of it should be below the surface.

 Focus point

Your setting should enhance and set the tone for your novel. Many places evoke an emotional response, and you need to aim to provoke an emotional response from your readers when they read about your world.

Snapshot

Worldbuilding is also about the emotions that come from
describing a place. Think of a place that you have a strong
emotional response to. This could be the place where you had
your first kiss, or your grandmother's house. Write an essay
describing that place, but focusing on the emotions it created
within you rather than just on its geographical setting. Did it make
you feel happy? Did it make you feel safe? Why? Think of what it
was in that place that created that emotion, and try to convey that
same sense to your reader. Try to make the reader understand why
that setting creates those emotions within you, and work to try to
create those emotions within the reader as they read the piece.

Edit

Go back to the write exercise where you focused on your
protagonist experiencing a setting through each of the five
senses. Have you paid enough attention to the mood that is
created by each of the senses, and by your character's emotional
response to the setting? If not, you need to go back and make
sure that the work conveys how each of the senses contributes to
the mood and the character's feelings.

Workshop

Look at your edited piece of writing about a setting and answer the following questions about it:

- Have you fully described the room considering every sense: sight, smell, taste, touch and hearing?
- Which of the senses have you focused on the most? Why have you focused on that sense the most?
- Which sense have you focused on the least? Why?
- Can you tell how the setting makes your character feel?
- How do you intend the reader to feel when they are reading about this setting?
- Do you think that you have achieved that successfully?
- If not, how can you improve on conveying this mood?
- Do you feel that this is an interesting piece of writing, or did you overwrite or underwrite?

Go back over your piece with these questions in mind and edit it as much as you can until you feel confident that you have achieved a strong standard of writing and description.

Next step

We have covered a lot in this chapter. You have learned the importance of worldbuilding, regardless of which type of genre you are writing in. You have learned how to plan a world, how to develop a set of rules for the world, and how to make sure that you do not give away too much information at once. You have also learned how to describe your world, focusing on using all of the senses, not just sight. You have also learned to consider how everything from geography to weather can affect the mood of a piece, creating a tone that can bring a piece of work to life. Finally, we have also looked at the importance of our emotional connection to settings and places, and how to convey that to the reader.

In the next chapter we are going to look at how to create and maintain suspense in your novel. Now you have got to grips with plotting, character and worldbuilding, it is important to look at how to maintain a gripping and interesting character arc for the novel.

6

Suspense, action and narrative arc

In the last chapter, we looked at worldbuilding and description in your YA novel. We are now going to look at how to make sure that your novel contains pace and has a defined and interesting narrative arc. In this chapter we will look at creating suspense, at foreshadowing plot points, at being active rather than passive, and at being disciplined at what makes it on to the page. By the end of this chapter you will be well on the way to writing an interesting and dynamic young adult novel.

Suspense

❝❞ Gus Van Sant

'The rules of suspense are that you do know, and you just don't know when. In the Hitchcock rules of suspense, you are supposed to know that there is a bomb on the bus that might blow up, and then it becomes very tense – but if you don't know that there's a bomb and it just blows up, then it's just a surprise.'

Suspense is a really important tool for the writer to master. Suspense is obviously integral when it comes to thrillers, mysteries or crime novels. But it is also integral in teen romances, or contemporary novels. Suspense does not just have to be about a bomb blowing up on a bus; it can also be whether our main character gets away with hiding her expulsion from her parents, or whether she gets together with the main character.

I like to think of writing suspense in the following way: there should be particular questions posed to the reader as they read the novel, and the novel should answer them satisfactorily by the end.

Here are some examples of what these questions are in famous YA novels:

- *We Were Liars* by E. Lockhart What happened to Cadence Sinclair that was so traumatic that she cannot remember it?
- *Eleanor & Park* by Rainbow Rowell Why is Eleanor's family so poor? Why is Eleanor hiding from her stepfather? Will she and Park succeed in hiding their relationship?
- *Twilight* by Stephenie Meyer Will Bella and Edward be together? Will Bella become a vampire? Will Bella escape the attempt on her life?
- *The Hunger Games* by Suzanne Collins Will Katniss survive? What happened to District 12? Will Peeta survive? Will they overthrow the despotic rulers?

As you can see, these questions vary wildly in scope, from questions about romance and domestic issues to questions about the fate of the world.

Key idea

You want to keep your reader guessing as they read the novel. We talked about CHARACTER in SETTING experiences CONFLICT to reach RESOLUTION. Suspense should absolutely support the CONFLICT and we should be left guessing as to how and why they will reach the RESOLUTION of the novel.

Snapshot

Make a list of three questions that readers will have about your novel, and how the questions will be answered by the novel's end. Think carefully about what will keep them guessing, and the mysteries which they will want to discover. Make sure that the answers feel satisfying to the reader, and that you have fully considered how they will get to these answers by the end of your book.

Focus point

Not all loose ends or plot points will be tied up by the end of a novel. Some novels are the first in a duology or trilogy, and these plot points will be solved later down the line. You need to make sure, however, that enough of the plot points are resolved by the end of book one so that the reader is satisfied, and actively wants to read on to the next book to find out more.

In the chapter on plot we talked about the three-act structure, and about a beat sheet, which should help you figure out what your story is actually about. All stories have some conflict at their heart. Some novels have a really big conflict such as that the world is going to end unless our heroine can find the sword of Ashara! Some have a more simple conflict: for example, our heroine is banned from having a boyfriend but is secretly in love with her best friend's boyfriend.

Will her strict parents find out? What will her best friend do when she finds out? You need to ensure that it is clear throughout what the conflict at the heart of your novel is. And once you have that figured out, you need to make sure that the rest of the novel works to build that conflict into a satisfying arc, creating and building suspense along the way.

The conflict of a novel can normally be summed up in a question you are asking of a reader. Consider these examples:

- *Divergent* In a world where everyone is categorized by one specific personality type, what happens when one girl is impossible to categorize?
- *The Perks of Being a Wallflower* Can shy and unpopular Charlie successfully complete his first year of high school, despite his traumatic past?

Snapshot

Try to sum up the central conflict of your novel in one question. Do not cheat and ask a very long question; instead, try to make it snappy and intriguing.

In our chapter on characters, we looked at the importance of an antagonist, and creating a layered and believable antagonist or antagonists. Sometimes, alongside your main antagonist, it can be interesting to have lesser antagonists, who also create conflict by getting in the way of the protagonist's aims. So perhaps the 'Big Bad' of your novel is a nuclear blast that your character needs to prevent from taking place. But perhaps along the way there can be conflict from an ex-friend who wants the blast to take place. Or from his older brother who wants him to stay away from trouble. Or from the girl he loves who is desperate for him to stay safe. Conflict can come in all shapes and sizes, from the epic world-changing conflict, to a smaller conflict between friends. But it is these plots and subplots that can elevate your novel into something that readers do not want to put down.

Key idea

It is important when writing a YA novel that you ensure that your conflict feels appropriate for your intended audience. We discussed earlier how often adult concerns are very different from young adult concerns, and this is something to consider when looking at the central conflict of your novel. It is important to consider whether or not your conflict feels in keeping with the age of the characters in your novel.

Write

Think back to when you were at school, and write an essay about a time in your life when you had conflict. This conflict could have been that you were concerned that you were going to fail an exam, it could have been a time you had to lie to a friend, or it could have been when you discovered that someone was being bullied and you had to decide whether to step in. Write a page detailing what happened, focusing on your emotions during this time.

Sara Zarr

'When the reader and one narrator know something the other narrator does not, the opportunities for suspense and plot development and the shifting of reader sympathies get really interesting.'

Snapshot

Make a list of five of your favourite films or novels. Write down what the key conflict was in each, and at least two subplots that took place within them.

Foreshadowing

Foreshadowing is a great tool that every writer should have in their arsenal. Foreshadowing is basically signposting major events in the novel for your reader and hinting to them about things to come in the text. It is important to foreshadow some of the major plot moments before they appear, so that the reader is suspecting them but is kept in suspense about how they will unfold, and when they will unfold. If we experience plot twists in real time, alongside the character, with no idea of what is to come, then you end up losing a lot of tension from the narrative.

Planning and plotting in advance can really help with this. If you know where your plot is going, and what is going to take place later in the novel, then you can make sure that you bed in some clues along the way for the reader to pick up on. Remember, however, not to put clues in place without actually making good on them in the novel. If you make a point of mentioning that a character is being glared at by a mysterious-looking man, the reader will need to find out who the mysterious-looking man is and why he is glaring at the character by the end of the novel.

Here are some examples of foreshadowing:

- **SET-UP:** Our protagonist bumps into a girl in the corridor and accidentally spills her books. He tries to help her but she angrily pushes him away, and gathers a weird-looking book before he can see it.
  PAY-OFF: We find out that the girl is our protagonist's sworn enemy, and that the book is a spell book detailing how she can remove his magical powers.
- **SET-UP:** Our protagonist has to have a meeting with his English teacher. He is nervous about it because of what happened 'last time'.
  PAY-OFF: The meeting goes badly and we discover that last time our protagonist lost his temper and swore at the teacher, and the teacher agreed not to tell his parents unless it happened again.
- **SET-UP:** The protagonist has her fortune read and the fortune-teller tells her that she will meet with true danger in the shape of a former love. Our protagonist laughs it off.
  PAY-OFF: Our protagonist meets an ex-boyfriend and agrees to go on a date with him, and he kidnaps her.

You can definitely overuse foreshadowing, which is something to be wary of because then it will start to feel less like a story and more like a police case. But the best novels use it as a way to keep the reader on their toes, giving us clues that make us eager to turn the pages and read on, so that we can find out about the pay-off to the set-ups.

Key idea

All of these tools and techniques are designed to increase tension. You want the reader to feel dramatic tension, and be eager to read on to discover what is going to happen to the characters. You are now practised at creating great characters and making us care about them, and you can use dramatic tension to reinforce that for the reader.

Narrative arc

Every writer needs to strike a balance between developing character and character arcs, and developing the narrative journey of the novel.

An example of a personal arc would be:

> Character A starts the novel as a bully, but when he discovers that he has a rare and life-limiting disease, he becomes a nicer person.

An example of the narrative journey of the novel in a wider context might be:

> Character A starts the novel as a bully, but discovers that he has a rare and life-limiting disease, genetically handed down from his father. He decides to set out to find his father, a famous geneticist, and find the keys to curing his illness and the keys to who made him who he is today.

The character arc might make for a fairly interesting read, but the narrative arc of the novel is what keeps us reading.

Another example could be:

> Character A has terrible stage fright. She must overcome her stage fright and discover her courage.

The wider arc, however, could be:

> Character A dreams of impressing her critical mother, as well as capturing the heart of the most popular boy in the school. When the school talent show arrives, she discovers that unless she takes part she will fail her drama module and lose her scholarship. As she tries to overcome her nerves, she discovers that someone is trying to thwart her at every turn. Can she discover who the mystery bully is, and do well enough to save her scholarship?

The character arc alone would be hard to keep interesting for an entire novel. Sixty thousand words just about the character's emotional journey would be a difficult sell for agent and reader alike. Creating a wider narrative arc, which complements and extends the character arc, makes this a much more compelling proposition for your readers.

A lot of first-time writers spend too long inside the character's heads, having them spend a lot of time reflecting on their own thoughts and feelings, or how they think and feel about the other characters in the novel. This can create a sense of stasis in the novel, whereas you want to be creating a sense of movement and impetus throughout, especially in a young adult novel. If we spend too much time in a character's head, it can lead to the novel feeling really passive. You need to strike a balance between external conflict and internal conflict – between action and emotion. A novel that is pure action would be very boring, but a novel that has too much focus on the character's interior world is just as boring.

 Focus point

There can certainly be scenes that are about us getting to know your characters, but try to space these out and try to reveal facts about your characters in a more organic way. A teen audience can be a critical audience, and you need to make sure that you keep their attention throughout.

Ken Follett

'For success, the author must make the reader care about the destiny of the principals, and sustain this anxiety, or suspense, for about 100,000 words.'

Snapshot

Come up with two or three ideas for character arcs and how they would tie in to wider narrative arcs. What is the character arc of your protagonist? What is the wider narrative arc of the novel? Do the two complement each other and tie together well? Why is this? If they don't, how can you rectify this to make the novel more satisfying to a reader?

Character

Creating characters we care about really helps to bring a novel to life. We need to invest in the characters in order to want to read about what happens to them. Sometimes, I read a novel that has a very boring character as the protagonist. When something dramatic happens to the character, it is a struggle for me to care. Sometimes a character can be so annoying that when bad things happen to them, I am actively pleased! That is not something that should happen in your novel.

We have already discussed how to make your characters come to life, but it bears repeating that the character should be a key aspect of creating a satisfying narrative arc. We should see your characters grow and change during the novel. The events that happen in the novel will have an impact on your characters. It would be a very boring novel if the characters were unchanged by the end of it. Especially in YA, we need to see the characters grow, and grow up. Whether they are affected by first love or by saving the world, we need to see them undergo changes of their own during the story.

Dan Brown

'I often will write a scene from three different points of view to find out which has the most tension and which way I'm able to conceal the information I'm trying to conceal. And that is, at the end of the day, what writing suspense is all about.'

The stakes

We have already looked at making sure the stakes of your novel make sense for the age of the characters, and make sense given the concept of your world. But it bears repeating and emphasizing that you need to be sure of what the stakes are for your characters when you begin a novel. The reader needs to know what the stakes are, too. What is at risk? What can the characters lose?

Sometimes the stakes are small. Perhaps the character might lose a scholarship, or fail their GCSEs, or fall out with their best friend. But sometimes the stakes are massive. Perhaps the character might die, or the world might end. We need to know what the stakes are – be they big or small – in order for us to invest in the narrative and want to keep reading on.

Think of the stakes in the following novels:

- *The Hunger Games* Will Katniss survive?
- *Harry Potter and the Deathly Hallows* Will Harry defeat Voldemort?
- *The Fire Sermon* Will Cass find the resistance island?
- *Half a King* Will Yarvi regain his kingdom and achieve vengeance?

The stakes all vary, but we know what they are from the beginning of the novel, and we therefore know what is at risk for the characters. This helps the reader care enough to read on.

Edit

Looking over your first chapter, considering what you have
learned in this chapter, examine the following:

- Is it suspenseful?
- Are your characters believable?
- Do you foreshadow the later events of the novel?
- Are your stakes clearly established from the start?

If necessary, rewrite this chapter until you feel that you can
answer 'yes' to all four questions with confidence.

Workshop

Look back over the first write exercise we did this chapter,
where you had to write about a conflict in your life. Answer the
following questions about it:

- Do your emotions come across?
- Is the reader invited to empathize with you?
- Is the conflict believable and compelling?
- Is the conflict an internal one or an external one?
- Is there an antagonist involved who helped create
  barriers to you achieving your aims?
- Did you describe what was at stake if you did not
  achieve what you wanted to?

If you have answered no to any of the questions, you need to
go back and look again at why, in order to resolve this.

In this chapter, we have looked creating suspense in your plot, focusing on foreshadowing, narrative arcs as well as personal arcs, and on the stakes at the heart of your novel. You have learned how to create a compelling plot, which obeys the rules of storytelling and which is interesting for readers.

In the next chapter we are going to look at writing rules and when to break them: taking as our starting point the key pieces of advice that writers are typically given. We are going to examine when to follow these pieces of advice closely, and when to ignore them. Through various exercises we will learn how to balance this advice, and not stick too religiously to any one way of thinking.

7

Writing rules and when to break them

We have covered a lot so far in this book, and you should have built up a bank of writing exercises that are helping you understand the discipline it takes to be a writer. We have looked at understanding your target market, coming up with ideas, plotting a novel, developing characters, and building your world and setting. You should have learned a lot so far, but there are still lots of tips and pointers to cover before you can become a published and successful author of young adult fiction.

In this section we will be looking at writing rules... and when to break them. There is a lot of advice out there for writers, and some of it has been so commonly repeated that it almost seems like law. Some of these pointers are fantastic and I thoroughly agree with them, some of them have parts that are true and parts that are false, and some you should take with a pinch of salt altogether! By the end of this chapter you will feel more confident about mastering language, dialogue and plot, and be well on your way to writing your young adult novel.

Writing habits

There is conflicting advice around what you need to become a writer. Some people swear by a laptop. They need something they can take with them to coffee shops to write on. Others need notebooks, to jot things down longhand. Others still say you need a whole writing space, preferably an office, in order to do your best work.

This is one rule that can definitely be broken. It would be wonderful if everyone could have their own study which they could write in, but unfortunately it just isn't that realistic for everyone. Similarly, dreaming of that expensive laptop can become a big timewaster. Rather than fixating on how you will write once you get the perfect 1) computer or 2) space, instead focus on getting started right now. Maybe it is on the computer in your library, maybe it is in the notes function on your mobile phone: wherever it is, just get in the habit of setting those thoughts down on paper.

And remember, what works for one person might not work for someone else. It is definitely not a one size fits all rule. Your friend might write best in longhand, in a library. You might find that a laptop in a busy coffee shop suits you best. But whatever it is, you just need to keep going, keep trying, and keep setting those words down.

You need to get into the habit of writing something as often as possible. My experience of writing this book was that if I wrote a little every day, I found it easier to pick up the thread of my thoughts and get cracking. The times when it was a week or two before I sat down to the document again made it much harder: I had to read back to remind myself of what I had already written. Writing needs to become a habit for you.

 ## Key idea

The one unbreakable rule for writing fiction is that you need to keep striving at it. If you don't get into the habit of sitting down each day, or each weekend, and putting words down on the paper or screen, then you are never going to get anywhere. Sometimes you can spend a lot of time procrastinating around writing, when you just need to sit down and do it.

NaNoWriMo

NaNoWriMo, otherwise known as National Novel Writing Month, was started in 1999 and runs in November every year. It is Internet based and sets out to challenge its participants to write 50,000 words of a novel in the month of November. The official website, nanowrimo.org, offers support tips and places where writers can meet to write together. Writers register before the month begins and have to submit their final word count in order to be validated and 'win NaNoWriMo'.

NaNoWriMo has its critics, as it focuses on getting words down rather than on quality. Lauren Miller, in *Salon*, wrote 'NaNoWriMo winners frequently ignore official advice about the importance of revision; editors and agents are already flinching in anticipation of the slapdash manuscripts they'll shortly receive.'[1] However, the success of NaNoWriMo definitely links to the advice I have already given of developing a writing routine, and writing often and consistently. NaNoWriMo does not give the reader the chance to doubt themselves: you have to write several thousand words a day to make your target, so you need to work hard and be focused.

The best NaNoWriMo winners will plan their novel in advance, so they know their plot, characters and world, and will then simply sit down and focus on getting the words down. At the end of the month, writers should revise and edit hard, expanding the word count where necessary, and making sure it is a polished book. Over 250 NaNoWriMo novels have been traditionally published, including Rainbow Rowell's *Fangirl* and Erin Morgenstern's *The Night Circus*.[2] NaNoWriMo can be a valuable way for writers to become used to setting down a solid word count every day, and building good writing habits.

[1] Lauren Miller, 'Better yet, DON'T write that novel', Salon.com http://www.salon.com/2010/11/02/nanowrimo/, accessed 22 December 2014.

[2] National Novel Writing Press, http://nanowrimo.org/press, accessed 22 December 2014.

Wattpad and fanfiction

Wattpad is a website that allows its registered users to post fanfiction, short stories, novels and fan-art for their original works. Often the most popular authors will upload a new chapter every day, or once a week. While these chapters may not be edited and polished, this can be a good way to build a habit of writing often: knowing that you have a fan base waiting for your next chapter can be a great motivator. People will also comment on your stories – which can help with the editorial process, or fixing issues within the text. Fanfiction writers also have to get into the habit of updating their stories regularly. Writing fanfiction – where you use another creator's characters in not-for-profit fiction – can be a great way to learn the craft of writing, and will hone your ability to tell a good story. Some published fanfiction writers include Naomi Novik and Cassandra Clare.

Spelling and grammar

Unless you have a very, very good reason not to – such as telling the book from the perspective of someone who struggles with English – your spelling should be impeccable. A novel that is littered with errors makes me think that the writer has not spent any time proofreading, and that they do not care about how I spend my time, and that they are too lazy to fix their own obvious errors. Get someone to proofread your work for you once you are done, and run a spell-check on it from your computer: it will help your work seem much more polished.

When it comes to grammar, you should, of course, play by the rules unless there is a very good reason not to do so. You should try not to write sentences that are too long, or too short. You should put a full stop where there seems to be a natural break in the sentence. The eye will pick up full stops, and it is interesting for the eye if you use sentences of differing lengths rather than all very short, or all very long. You should not rely too much on commas, or have long, unwieldy sentences.

GRAMMAR IN DIALOGUE

In UK style, quotation marks should be single, and a quotation within dialogue should be inside double quotation marks (the reverse applies in the US style, though publishers' house style also varies). You should make sure that this is consistent throughout.

You should use a comma between the dialogue and the words used to identify the speaker:

'Make sure that you use grammar correctly,' Juliet told the authors.

Full stops and commas always go inside the quotation marks:

'This is correct,' Juliet said. 'This is not correct', she explained.

What happens if you have dialogue divided by a dialogue tag? In this instance you need to place a second comma after the tag, and after any words that come between the tag and the continuation of the sentence:

'Don't worry,' Juliet said, 'you will find that this gets easier to remember the more you try it.'

When you are illustrating that another character has interrupted your speaker, you should use a dash, to show that their speech has been cut off. And when a character trails off at the end of a sentence, you should use an ellipsis:

'I don't know how to—'

'Yes, you do know how to punctuate dialogue correctly. Or at least I hope you do...'

You should always begin a new paragraph each time a new character is speaking.

If your character is asking a question, the question mark should go before the closed quotation marks.

Obeying these rules, unless you have a very good reason not to do so, is an important part of the writing process.

Joan Didion

'Grammar is a piano I play by ear. All I know about grammar is its power.'

BREAKING GRAMMAR RULES

Generally speaking, you need to play by the rules. However, there are some notable exceptions where people play around with their grammar in order to create something rather different from the norm.

Some writers tell their story from the perspective of someone who might not always use correct English, in order to create a powerful voice and flavour to the novel.

A great example of this is the *Chaos Walking* trilogy by Patrick Ness, which is told from the perspective of Todd and is peppered with abbreviations, misspellings and incorrect grammar usage:

> The first thing you find out when yer dog learns to talk is that dogs don't got nothing much to say. About anything.[3]

Similarly, *Push* by Sapphire is told in dialect. It is told from the perspective of an illiterate 16-year-old girl, and the writer does not always obey the laws of spelling and grammar, in order to create a believable voice:

> Listen baby, Muver love you. Muver not dumb. Listen baby: ABCDEFGHIJKLMNOPQRSTUVWXYZ.

> Thas the alphabet. Twenty-six letters in all. Them letters make up words. Them words everything.[4]

In both of these cases, not following strict grammatical rules definitely adds to how interesting the voice is, and how readable the novel is. However, it is important to note that both of these novels are exceptions. There is also a big difference between having decided ahead of time that you are going to tell your story from the perspective of an illiterate character, or someone who speaks in dialect, and just being a bit lazy when writing. A deliberate stylistic choice is one thing: a lazy decision is quite another!

---

[3] Patrick Ness, *The Knife of Never Letting Go* (Walker Books, 2014).

[4] Sapphire, *Push: A Novel* (Vintage, 1998).

Focus point

There are generally accepted rules of spelling and grammar, and it is important to follow these as much as possible. However, as demonstrated above, there are some deliberate stylistic choices that contravene these rules. If you have planned ahead, and are confident that this is the way forward, do not be afraid to experiment.

Snapshot

Think about something you witnessed this week that stuck in your mind. It could be an odd-looking dog; it could be an annoying delay on your commute to work. Write two paragraphs explaining what happened, but telling it entirely in dialogue. Person 1 (you) and person 2 (whoever you choose) are conversing – they are interjecting and asking questions as you relate the anecdote. Make sure that you are using dialogue grammar correctly throughout.

Mark Twain, in a letter to a 12-year-old boy who had written to him

'I notice that you use plain, simple language, short words and brief sentences. That is the way to write English – it is the modern way and the best way. Stick to it; don't let fluff and flowers and verbosity creep in. When you catch an adjective, kill it. No, I don't mean utterly, but kill most of them – then the rest will be valuable. They weaken when they are close together. They give strength when they are wide apart. An adjective habit, or a wordy, diffuse, flowery habit, once fastened upon a person, is as hard to get rid of as any other vice.'

'Write what you know'

'Write what you know' is one of the most common pieces of writing advice you can hear. But is it a rule that should never be broken?

I think that the world of fiction would be very boring indeed if people only ever wrote what they precisely knew. We would have no dragons in *Eragon*, no dinosaurs in *Jurassic Park*, no spaceships in *Ender's Game*. However, there is definitely something to be learned from 'write what you know', even if we do not accept that it is always the right thing to do.

You can and should use your own experiences and emotions to bring your characters to life. For example, your main character's dog has just died, and you remember the loss of your beloved cat when you were eleven. You can cast back to these memories and use them to make this story seem more believable, and more moving. You never went off to fight in a magical war, but you can remember what it was like to leave your family and friends behind when you headed off to university, so use these memories and emotions to bring your story to life and make it feel truly realistic for the reader.

If you can research something, then you definitely should research it. If your novel is set in the world of competitive show-jumping, even if you have never sat on a horse in your life, you should do as much research as you possibly can so that in some ways you are writing what you know. Poor research shows, and it can seem jarring to the reader, as discussed when we looked at planning your novel and worldbuilding.

If you have actually experienced something yourself, you can definitely bring a wealth of feeling and knowledge to the topic. You can talk about a friend dying of cancer with a lot of compassion and understanding if that is something that actually happened to you. Or if your novel is about a teenage chess prodigy, and you were a teenage chess prodigy, the chances are that you will be able to bring impeccable research and real insight into the writing process.

There are some great examples out there of writers writing what they know and creating excellent books. For example:

- *Geek girl* by Holly Smale is about a young girl who is scouted by a modelling agency – this is what happened to the author when she was a teenager.
- Judy Blume's novels are about the experience of growing up as a young American teenager. She brought her real-life experiences to bear on her characters.

However, if you only ever write what you know, then some of the most interesting YA novels out there would never have existed. For example, we would never have been introduced to the romance between Korean-American Park and American Eleanor if Rainbow Rowell had felt she couldn't write someone from a different culture in *Eleanor & Park*. We would never have met Katniss Everdeen, or Hazel Lancaster, or Clary Fray if their creators had only stuck to creating people who were exactly like them.

Key idea

You absolutely should bring your personal emotional experiences to bear on what you write, and research your novel. But you do not always need to 'write what you know' – some of the most interesting and creative pieces of work come about from writing on topics very different from those you know a lot about.

Snapshot

Write a scene from the perspective of your protagonist, which deals with a situation you have never dealt with before. Perhaps they have been expelled from school, or they have broken up a fight, or their elder brother has been arrested. Draw on your own personal experiences to make it come to life, and for it to feel believable.

'You need a title before you begin'

You might think that it is essential to decide on a title for your novel at the outset – and definitely before you find an agent. A great title can absolutely help crystallize your thoughts and focus your book, and, as we have discussed, it can really help you understand the kind of book you are writing. A great title can be a fantastic boon to the writer, especially early in the process. But that does not mean by any stretch that you should sit around waiting for an excellent title to strike you like a bolt from the blue, and that you should put off writing until it does. If you cannot come up with a title, you should start writing your novel anyway, and see if anything springs to mind during the process.

Some novels have a very different title from the one they started with when they come to be published. Here are some examples:

- *To Kill a Mockingbird* by Harper Lee was originally called 'Atticus'.
- *The Lord of the Flies* by William Golding was called 'Strangers from Within' when found in Faber & Faber's slush pile.
- Frances Hodgson Burnett's *The Secret Garden* had the working title of 'Mistress Mary'.

Some novels that I have worked on were called something very different when I first saw them in my slush pile. Not having the right title did not stop me signing them; it was just something we worked on together before finding something we felt was the strongest representation for the book that we could have.

- *Banished* by Liz de Jager (published by Tor) was originally called 'The Blackwood Chronicles'.
- *The Last Summer of Us* by Maggie Harcourt (published by Usborne) was originally titled 'The Dead Mothers' Club'.

We come back to the first piece of advice, which is to just keep on writing. Even if you don't think you have the right title yet, you should keep on writing because you will get there in the end. Try brainstorming ideas around the novel's themes, the characters and the settings of the novel. You might be surprised by how quickly something will jump out at you when you keep working at it.

'Never use a prologue'

Prologues get a bad rap these days. A prologue (from the Greek *prologos*) is an opening to a story that gives background information before the story begins. Some prologues do not make sense until later in the story. Some are told from the perspective of a different character to the main character. Some give a backdrop and an exposition of the world we are in.

I often get asked, 'How do you feel about prologues?' and have heard some agents say that they will not accept submissions that use prologues. Elmore Leonard advises, in his top ten tips for writers, that you should avoid them.

However, some prologues work well to establish a sense of menace or a sense of place, or they tantalize us with information that we cannot quite understand yet but which will become clear later in the text.

Here are my top five things to look out for when considering if your prologue is truly necessary or not:

1 Do not use a prologue because you are worried that the opening chapters of your novel are boring. If the opening chapters of your novel are boring, you need to address that by rewriting them. Sticking a dramatic prologue at the beginning of them is not the way forward.

2 Do not use a prologue as a big exposition dump. Some prologues are just an excuse for the writer to put a load of background information in one place. Cut it, if that is the case.

3 If your prologue is really long, I would question whether it is a prologue at all, or if it is a first chapter by another name.

4 If your prologue is told from the perspective of a character who we never hear from again in the novel, that can be very annoying for the reader, who expects this character to appear again somewhere in the narrative. Question your motivations for doing this, if this is the case.

5 Do not use the prologue as a vehicle to give us a lot of weighty backstory about a character. Ask yourself whether we need to know all of this information before we meet a character, or whether you can share that information in a more organic way rather than spending a prologue explaining why the main character is the way she is, before we cut to the main action.

If it slows down the text, does not add anything to the plot, and is an excuse for you to smuggle in extraneous information, you need to cut it. Be brave, and delete that text.

Key idea

Prologues are absolutely not an instant turn-off for either publisher or reader, but you need to have a very good reason to use one. Often, a prologue can put you in danger of relying on it to do some heavy lifting for you, rather than working out those issues in the main text.

Adjectives and adverbs

Stephen King

'Any word you have to hunt for in a thesaurus is the wrong word. There are no exceptions to this rule.'

Adjectives are one of the traditional eight English parts of speech. They are describing words, which are used to qualify or modify a noun. Adverbs are words that modify a verb, another adverb or an adjective. They tell us how something has been done. Used sparingly, they can be effective, and can help bring to life a character, scene or setting. When overused, however, they serve as a distraction, and they can turn your prose from punchy to paunchy.

Look at the following paragraph and circle every adjective that has been used:

> The tall girl walked along the dark, purple corridor, playing with her long, curly hair as she went. The floor was sticky as she walked along it, which made her wrinkle her pointy nose. The walls were bare, and shadowy. She wanted to go back to her small, cosy dormitory, with its colourful walls and snug and warm bed. She wondered if the caretaker's cat – fat, curly, old Jenks – would be lying on the patterned bed even now. She started walking quickly, hoping to get this dull errand over and done with.

There are 19 adjectives in the sentence:

- The girl is **tall** and has **long, curly** hair and a **pointy** nose.
- The corridor is **dark** and **purple**, with **bare** and **shadowy** walls and a **sticky** floor.
- Her dormitory is **small, cosy,** and **colourful**.
- Her bed is **snug, warm** and **patterned**.
- The cat is **fat, curly** and **old**.
- The errand is **dull**.

What you might well find is that rather than helping you imagine the girl and the school, you have such an overload of adjectives that you cannot actually picture it at all.

If we had used adverbs in the sentence, it might have become even more confusing:

> The very tall girl walked along the dark, purple corridor, playing with her somewhat long, curly hair as she went. The floor was sticky as she walked along it, which made her wrinkle her pointy nose. The walls were bare, and shadowy. She wanted to go back to her small, cosy dormitory, with its colourful walls and snug and warm bed. She wondered if the caretaker's cat – fat, quite curly, old Jenks – would be lying on the patterned bed even now. She started walking quickly, hoping to get this dull errand over and done with.

We know that she is very tall, with quite long hair, and that the cat is quite curly. But all that this serves to do is increase the word count without actually adding much – if anything – to the writing.

What happens when you use too many adjectives is that the reader stops paying attention to all of them, as there are too many to pay attention to at once. Rather than increasing the feeling of a place, you end up leaving the reader feeling very confused.

Key idea

A common error with first-time novels is that they rely on too many adjectives, and use strings of adjectives. Using adjectives sparingly makes them much more effective and can really help with your descriptions.

That is not to say that you should never use adjectives and adverbs, however, as they can prove to be a powerful tool.

Consider this sentence:

> She leaned in towards him and their lips met. They began to kiss. He pulled away, and put his hand on her shoulder. 'We shouldn't have done that.'

This is a sentence that currently tells us very little. We do not know the context of how and why they are kissing, or why he says that they shouldn't have done it. Now try it with some adverbs and adjectives:

> She leaned hesitantly in towards him and their lips met. They slowly began to kiss. He pulled away reluctantly, and put his trembling hand on her shoulder. 'We shouldn't have done that.'

Using only three adverbs and one adjective, we now know that she was hesitant and that their kiss – presumably a first kiss now – was slow. He was reluctant to stop kissing her, and his hand is trembling with emotion when they stop.

Or, using four different adverbs and adjectives, we can put a completely different spin on things:

> She leaned suddenly in towards him and their lips met. They began to kiss, momentarily. He pulled away quickly, and put a firm hand on her shoulder. 'We shouldn't have done that.'

In this version she surprises him with a kiss, and they only kiss for a moment. He feels embarrassed by what she has instigated.

Using more adverbs for emphasis can also increase the impact:

> She leaned in towards him and their lips met very slowly. They began to kiss, a little awkwardly. He pulled away, and put his hand on her shoulder. 'We shouldn't have done that.'

We know that they kissed very slowly, and that their kiss was slightly awkward, and perhaps this is why he pulls away.

 Snapshot

Try this for yourself, using four adverbs and adjectives, to change the meaning of the piece. Do one version with a happy feeling, one that invokes a sad mood, and one that seems passionate.

However, if we overuse adjectives and adverbs, we can end up destroying any meaning in the piece:

> She leaned in quickly and suddenly towards him and their parted lips met. They began to kiss, passionately and aggressively. He pulled away very slowly, and put his strong, shaking hand on her tense shoulder. 'We shouldn't have done that.'

Using too many modifiers can completely change the feel of a piece, and not for the better.

Similes and metaphors

Similes and metaphors, when used sparingly, can certainly add flavour and flare to a piece of writing. But, and I know I keep returning to this word, they need to be used sparingly, not filling the pages so that the piece reads like a primary-school-level essay.

Similes are rhetorical figures of speech that compare two things that are alike in some way, and typically the words 'like' or 'as' are used.

Some very well-known similes are:

- as busy as a bee
- as cute as a button
- as cold as ice
- as blind as a bat
- as cunning as a fox.

Metaphors are figures of speech used to make an analogous comparison between two things, without using the words 'like' or 'as'.

Some common metaphors are:

- all the world's a stage
- she is a night owl
- he is a peacock
- America is a melting pot
- broken heart
- I'm feeling blue.

Key idea

If you stop to consider how many similes and metaphors pepper conversation, you will be better equipped to avoid clichés in your novel.

Similes can definitely make something more interesting, and they can be used really successfully for comic effect, for example:

> 'Fate is like a strange, unpopular restaurant filled with odd little waiters who bring you things you never asked for and don't always like.' (Lemony Snicket)

or:

> 'Delly lost her temper at Peeta over how he treated you. She got very squeaky. It was like someone stabbing a mouse with a fork repeatedly.' (Suzanne Collins, *Mockingjay*)

Some similes and metaphors are unusual, which also makes them stand out and helps them add flavour:

> 'He'd felt like a jack-o-lantern for the past few days, as if his guts had been yanked out with a fork and dumped in a heap while a grinning smile stayed plastered on his face.' (Cassandra Clare, *City of Ashes*)

or:

> 'The wind blowing through my ripped clothes was so cold that I felt like a Percysicle.' (Rick Riordan, *The Titan's Curse*)

However, there are some common similes and metaphors that are so overused that you just feel that the writer has not tried very hard. Sometimes it seems as if the writer has strayed into cliché, which should absolutely be avoided.

Key idea

You should think about similes, metaphors, adjectives and adverbs as ways to add depth and layers to your writing, without overly relying on them.

Edit

The following piece has some very common similes and metaphors in it. I want you to edit the piece so that you get rid of the common similes and metaphors, and replace them with other, more unusual ones. You don't have to replace every single one: some of them you can simply delete, but try to replace at least three with something different. Be as creative as you can be in this, and really push the bar when it comes to the descriptors you are using.

Princess Tyara grimaced as she looked at her reflection: 'You look like death,' she said to herself. It was hardly surprising; she normally slept like a log but lately she had been tossing and turning all night long. Since the war with the elves had broken out, her face was constantly tight with anxiety, and she was as wound up as a freshly coiled spring.

'Princess!' She heard her nanny's voice calling for her, her voice as clear as a bell in the echoing chamber.

'Coming!' she called back, but perhaps more loudly than she intended. Her nanny greeted her with the words, 'There was no need to bellow like a bull, your Majesty.'

Write

So far, we have looked at a lot of writing rules, and when they can be broken, and we have focused on description. Look back to the character notes you worked on in Chapter 6. I want you to write a page-long essay describing your main character, using no more than one adjective or adverb per sentence, and no more than two similes or metaphors. Really focus on how much information you can convey with the fewest words, and only use modifiers where they are really necessary. Try to build up a clear picture of the character as creatively as possible, using other devices where necessary to give the same information.

Purple prose

The term 'purple prose' comes from a reference by the Roman poet Horace to 'purpureus pannus'. Horace wrote in his *Ars poetica* (lines 14–21):

> Your opening shows great promise, and yet flashy
> purple patches; as when describing
> a sacred grove, or the altar of Diana,
> or a stream meandering through fields,
> or the river Rhine, or a rainbow;
> but this was not the place for them. If you can
> realistically render
> a cypress tree, would you include one when
> commissioned to paint
> a sailor in the midst of a shipwreck?

The term has now commonly come to describe writing that is excessively descriptive, and overuses rhetorical flourishes to create a very flowery passage.

A normal sentence might read:

> She was certain that she was going to fail her Maths GCSE, and it scared her.

Purple prose might read:

> She was absolutely positively 100 per cent sure that she was going to abysmally and terribly fail her nemesis, her white whale: her Maths GCSE. The thought of it struck fear into her heart, making her pulse quicken and her palms sweat, causing panicky breaths and the certainty that her life as she knew it was over. Her knees knocked and she felt that she might throw up at any moment.

While the latter paragraph could be used to show the character's histrionic tendencies, in general, this sort of over-the-top writing is to be avoided.

A common symptom of purple prose is very long words, which you would be unlikely to use in normal speech. As Stephen King said, if you need to go and look it up in a thesaurus first, then there is no way you should be using it! He is absolutely right. Often, simpler words are best.

Focus point

Like anything, purple prose in short doses where there is a reason for it, be it for humour or to highlight a character's frame of mind, can work, but it is something to watch out for in your novel because it can be irritating and distracting for the reader.

Snapshot

Look at the following sentence and replace the modifiers and figures of speech with simpler ones, or cut them out entirely where you feel it will work better that way.

Tom peered surreptitiously around the corner and ostentatiously gestured for the anxiety-stricken Sally to follow him towards the toweringly haunting mansion that loomed from tendrils of shadow like an ogre from a child's nightmare.

When I receive novels that are written in purple prose, I find it difficult to pay attention to what is going on and I start to skim-read the sentences. Often, I can get to the end of the first chapter and realize that, actually, nothing has happened; there has just been a lot of description of a place or person with no forward movement of the plot.

'Kill your darlings'

Samuel Johnson

'Read over your compositions, and wherever you meet with a passage which you think is particularly fine, strike it out.'

I have been known to tell writers that if they write a particular phrase and feel overly fond of it then they should delete it at once, but is it always fair to say that writers should 'kill their darlings'?

It was William Faulkner who coined the expression, but he is certainly not the only writer to warn against being self-indulgent in novels. From Samuel Johnson to Stephen King, it has become a really well-known refrain. Sometimes writers take it to mean that they should literally kill off their characters, but that is not what it means at all. You should think seriously about your characters, why they are there and what they add to the novel, but you don't need to take the expression so literally.

There is definitely some truth in the instruction, however. Some writers, especially those writing later books in a trilogy or series, take a lot of enjoyment from their characters and can be known to write some fairly self-indulgent chapters which are their characters talking about their emotions, or their past, in ways that add very little to the plot or colour of the novel.

I tell my creative writing students that they should ask themselves: does this add to the plot, or add to our understanding of character or setting? If not, why is it here?

Sometimes, your 'darlings' might actually be pieces that really add to the novel and, by all means, please keep those in. But often a particular scene you love, or even just a paragraph of description which you particularly enjoy, adds very little to the novel and is in fact just slowing down the pace. That is definitely something that you need to watch out for.

You need to be disciplined as a writer, and be strict with yourself, and make sure that everything you write has a purpose in building your plot and creating a sense of a journey and an arc in the novel. Often, your favourite pages are those where the reader's attention is likely to wander off.

It is very difficult for a writer to be truly objective about their work and you need that objectivity and distance in order to be able to see the good from the bad in your writing. My advice is to put your book away for a while, and then look at it again in a month or so, when those unnecessary flourishes will suddenly seem very obvious to you. We will look at this in greater detail in the chapter on editing.

'Show, don't tell'

Showing, not telling, is an incredibly common piece of advice for writers. In fact, you will have completed some exercises in this book already that pertain to showing rather than telling. However, as we discussed then, there are some occasions when it is preferable to tell rather than to show in a novel. Telling is literally reporting to us what has happened, whereas showing is letting the reader figure it out for themselves through the character's actions, or through dialogue. Telling can, however, occasionally be useful. Sometimes it is easier to tell us a big piece of backstory in a few words, rather than tie yourself in knots trying to convey it rather than just saying it.

For example, saying 'the meteor which hit Earth five years ago had resulted in a lot of mutants' is easier than trying to have the characters refer to the mutants, the meteor, and how long ago it hit. That isn't to say that you should always reach for the lazy shorthand. Sometimes it is far more elegant or far more suspenseful for the reader to have to guess at why the mutants exist, and have us forming our own theories during the text.

Sometimes, too, a quick and easy description of someone's looks is OK. You can sometimes tell us that a character is handsome, or unkind, or very tall you don't need to always be looking at ways to write around that. However, too much telling can end up making a novel feel like a list, or a very detailed schedule.

Compare the following passage:

> Conor woke up, just before his alarm went off at 8 a.m. He yawned, stretched, got out of bed and got into the shower. After singing in the shower, as a warm-up for his audition, he got ready for school. He got to school on time and had his audition at 10 a.m. and he managed to get the lead role.

with this one:

> Conor woke up before his alarm went off, which was
> unsurprising considering how much rested on today. He couldn't
> be late. He had to get that part. He spent his time in the shower
> warming up his voice, singing snatches of his audition song, even
> though he knew the words by heart now. He had been waiting
> for this moment all year. He was going to get the lead, he just
> knew it. He couldn't fail. Debbie would never speak to him again
> if he did.

The second version gives us much more insight into the character's
emotions, and makes us invest much more in his audition. Look
through your own work and consider where you have perhaps
shown us too much and also where you have told us too much.

Write

Write a page expanding on the passage above, telling us more
about Conor's story. Focus on showing us his emotional state,
creating an interesting setting – maybe he goes to school in a
spaceship or he lives at some time in the past. Be creative, and
work hard to ensure that you are not relying too much on telling, or
showing us when it would be easier and quicker to tell.

Workshop

Look back at the piece of work you have just written. Ask yourself the following questions:

How many similes/metaphors do you use?

- How many adjectives do you use?
- Could you cut back on them, and give the same information in a different way?
- Are there any particular lines that you enjoy? Why? Do they need to be there?
- Are your spelling and grammar consistent throughout?
- Do you create a strong sense of character?
- What is the tone of the piece you have written?

Edit the piece based on any strengths and weaknesses you have identified through answering these questions, until you feel that you can justify each stylistic decision you have made.

Next step

In this chapter we have looked at common writing rules and tips, and you have honed your use of description, and of showing rather than telling. You have learned when to listen to advice, and when to discard it as unhelpful.

In the next chapter you will be learning how to edit your novel. We will be identifying key areas to look out for, how to apply these writer's 'rules' to making your novel as strong as possible, and how you know if your novel is finally finished. The chapter will contain proven techniques to help you create a polished final draft of your YA novel.

8

How to edit your novel

In this book we have worked on various edit and workshop exercises, which are designed to get you to think critically about your own work. In this chapter we are going to be looking at editing your whole novel. Once you have typed the final full stop, and written the words 'The End', I am afraid to say that the finish line is not yet in sight. There is a big difference between a finished novel and a polished, edited, tautly written novel. Editing is a very separate skill to writing. Some writers are excellent editors, whereas others can really struggle with the process of editing and critiquing their work. However, the difference between good novels and great ones, or even bad novels and good ones, is in the editing.

Stephen King, in his seminal 'On Writing', reflects on advice given to him by a creative writing teacher called John Gould: '"When you write a story, you're telling yourself the story," he said. "When you rewrite, your main job is taking out all the things that are not the story."'

In this chapter we are going to look at ways to get rid of extraneous words, pieces of information the reader does not need, and anything else which simply works to slow down the story. You need to make sure that your story is always moving forwards, not taking little interesting scenic routes away from your destination: the ending. In this chapter we will be expanding some of the exercises from earlier in the book, and learning when it is time to start editing, editing best practice, and when to finally stop redrafting your book.

When to edit

You will hear conflicting advice on when to edit your novel, from writers and creative writing teachers. Some people recommend editing as you go along, so that after each chapter is finished you then start the process of editing that chapter. Others recommend editing in stages, so that once you have finished the first quarter, or half, you then edit the text before you go on. On creative writing courses it is common to workshop text. For each class, a student will prepare a section or a chapter, and in class the other students will offer their criticisms and suggestions to the author so that they can take those on board as they continue to write the piece.

In my opinion, the best time to edit is once you have a complete first draft of your book in front of you.

 Dominick Dunne

'The best advice on writing was given to me by my first editor, Michael Korda, of Simon and Schuster, while writing my first book. "Finish your first draft and then we'll talk," he said. It took me a long time to realize how good the advice was. Even if you write it wrong, write and finish your first draft. Only then, when you have a flawed whole, do you know what you have to fix.'

If you are continuously editing as you go, you often end up damaging the flow of the novel. You also can get into the mindset of no longer seeing your novel as one continuous whole but instead only in small, bite-sized sections. Those individual sections might work, but you are writing a young adult novel, not a collection of vignettes. You need to make sure that your novel hangs together as a continuous story, rather than feeling episodic.

Key idea

Your novel is about one continuous journey, or arc, so make sure that you have finished it before you start to tinker with it and edit it. You will find it easier to identify its strengths as well as weaknesses once you have a whole novel in front of you.

The importance of finishing your book

I always request manuscripts to be finished and edited before authors submit to me, even though they are only submitting the first three chapters. This is because a story changes radically in the telling. You might begin your story thinking that it is a sweet coming-of-age romance, but halfway through you realize that actually, your main character's relationship is toxic, and it becomes a drama as she tries to escape from the clutches of her abusive boyfriend. Sometimes the changes are not as major as those, but they still require you to rethink earlier sections of your book. Perhaps you realize once you reach the end that one of the characters does not make much sense, or that there is a plot hole you need to fix. Having the book in front of you as a whole means that you can move around the manuscript fixing these issues once you see them.

If you edit only on a micro level rather than on a macro level, you might pick up smaller issues but not the bigger ones that affect the whole overarching structure of your book.

I mentioned earlier the 'word vomit' draft, but it bears repeating. The best advice you can have as a writer is just to keep writing, to write as much as possible, as often as you can, and to get those words down on the page. Once you have your completed 70,000 or 90,000 words, then you can consider them as a whole, and begin to view it as a completed novel rather than a section of chapters.

Time and distance

One of the best ways to begin to edit is to finish your novel and to put it away for at least a month. Maybe in that time you work on something else, or you start reading other novels, or you just take a complete break from writing. The important thing is to give your mind a rest from those characters and that story, so the story has time to settle. Then you should take the novel out and read it as a whole. Don't worry too much at this stage about getting the red pen out and embarking on big edits; instead, you should focus on reading it as if it is any other book you would read. Let the story wash over you, and see how you feel about it as you read it.

 Focus point

Read your novel in a format different from the one you wrote it in, if possible. If you wrote it on screen, print it off and read it as printed paper. Or put it on to an e-reading device and read it as you travel to and from work. That act, even though it is a simple one, will help create distance between you and the text you have created.

No one has ever written a first draft and had it traditionally published exactly as it is, and there is a good reason for this. If you are disciplined and write, say, 2,000 words a day, there is every chance that at the end of three months you will have a novel. But among those 2,000 words you wrote each day, there are probably words which are unnecessary, motivations which do not make sense, chapters which go nowhere, and dialogue which does not sound realistic at all. It is highly unlikely that those 2,000 words a day were all precisely the right words at precisely the right time.

When I wrote this book, I took my own advice, which is how I know it works. I wrote the entire thing, put it away for a month, and then put it onto my e-reading device to read. On my commute to and from work each week I read it as if I were reading a published non-fiction book. Bits of it were good, bits of it would have been good if I had told them in half the time I took, and some bits made absolutely no sense. I also noticed points where I had written 'attribute this quote' or 'what does this mean?' or 'try this exercise first and then rewrite', which I had flagged during the writing process. That can certainly be a useful way to signpost to yourself issues that you might otherwise forget about.

Once I read the new draft, I also started to look at how it hung together as a whole. Yes, there were chapters that worked on their own, but they did not link effectively to the next chapter. Think of a novel, or a book, as an extended argument. You are building on what has gone before continuously, leading towards a satisfying and appropriate climax which makes sense in the context of what you have already written.

Write

Once you have put your novel away for a month and then read it through, I want you to take out a fresh piece of paper and write a 750-word review of your book, as if you were a critic. Spend a few lines summarizing the plot and genre of the book, then analyse its strengths as well as its weaknesses. If you finish it and do not think that there are any weaknesses, then you are a one-of-a-kind prodigy, and you need to go back and read it again after another month has passed.

What makes your book unique? Are the characters believable? Did you want to know what happened at the end? Did it follow a traditional three-act structure and build towards a climax? Does it have a satisfying conclusion or does it leave you wanting more? Try to analyse objectively its strengths, as well as looking at the areas which need work.

I always encourage authors to read their work aloud when they are trying to edit their work. It is very common to use certain key words or phrases over and over again. I have one author who uses 'moreover' constantly, and another who had someone shrugging 42 times in her manuscript. When you read your book aloud it becomes much more apparent when you are using the same word repeatedly. It is also easy to see if your dialogue rings true when you read it aloud. Does it flow? Does it make sense? Are you using too many long sentences, or getting bogged down in too many short and punchy sentences? See if it flows, or if it is difficult to read. See which paragraphs you want to skip over, and which manage to keep your attention glued from start to finish.

Focus point

You should always have in mind whether your YA novel is appropriate and interesting for your target market. When you are reading it through before editing, always have in the back of your mind whether your characters sound convincing for the intended age range, and whether they speak the way teenagers really do speak.

Snapshot

Ask a friend to read aloud a passage of dialogue with you from your novel. You take one part, and they take the other. Does it flow? Does it make sense as a conversation? Does it add to the sense of character? Does it feel appropriate for the target age range?

Bravery and new drafts

Revising a novel can sound like a boring and thankless task. Surely getting the words down is the hard part? Wrong! Getting the words down is definitely a hard part, and you should be very proud of yourself for having got this far. But if you stopped now, it would be like a sprinter stopping dead halfway through the race and still expecting to somehow be at the finish line. The revising process can actually be hugely rewarding, too. As you read your novel, you should feel excitement about its potential. You might also find yourself thinking of new ideas or ways to resolve issues that you had the first time around.

Don't be afraid to delete chapters, and insert wholly new ones. I advise writers to save one document as 'Draft 1'. Then copy and paste it in its entirety into a new document saved as 'Draft 2'. You can then change it as much as you like, but you are not losing any of the work that went into Draft 1. Perhaps, as you finish Draft 2, you realize that actually you cut too many scenes and it does not work as well now. But Draft 1 will be saved as a separate document, so you have definitely not lost those for ever. It is very freeing once you know that these changes are not set in concrete. You can easily change your mind as you go on, and you do not have to worry that you have lost some really good edits or phrases, just because you are editing them out this time around.

Focus point

As you read your novel, don't forget to take time to savour the good moments as well as the bad. There will probably be points where you think 'Oh, wow, this is interesting', and some of my authors have cried when rereading particularly emotional scenes in their own novel. Let yourself enjoy those moments and feel proud of them.

Structural edits

Once you have read your novel through for the first time, and written your review of it, it is time to think seriously about editing it. Most novels need a structural edit first of all.

Structural editing, or 'macro editing', focuses on the bigger picture issues within a novel. You should be looking at the following issues:

- **Pace** Does the story have pace throughout? Are there moments where the pace drops off and the novel slows? How can you address that? Do you cut those sections, or work on them to make them necessary to the story arc?
- **Character** Do your characters make sense? Do you care about the characters and invest in them? Often, character motivation is a big issue to address in edits. Often, a character will clearly be doing something because the plot needs them to do so, rather than because it is in keeping with their character's needs or personality. You need to make sure that your characters make

sense, and that their actions spring from logical, well-thought-through decisions on your part, rather than purely because the plot necessitates them acting in a particular way.

- **World** Does the worldbuilding work? Are you giving us enough information so that the setting makes sense? Are there any questions that the reader might have, which you need to find a way to answer in the text?

- **Appropriate for YA** Are there points where the novel drifts away from its core audience? How do you go about fixing them?

- **Plot** Does the plot make sense? Do the characters act in a way that fits the setting? Does the plot feel logical and rational? Is there a consistent internal logic to the setting, so that we know the rules of this world?

- **Narrative arc** Is the arc of your story interesting? Do your characters start in one place (this can be an emotional place as well as a physical one) and go on a journey to reach somewhere else? Do you stay interested in their journey throughout?

- **Structure** Does the novel have a clear beginning, middle, and end? Is there an inciting incident, clear conflict and suspense, and a satisfying climax?

- **Style** Is there too much purple prose? Do you spend too long describing things rather than having things happen? Do the characters talk in a way that feels believable? Is your style consistent throughout? Does your dialogue work?

- **Point of view** Are there too many points of view? Is one POV stronger than the others? Why? Do the voices for your POVs feel authentic and in keeping with the rest of the novel?

- **Dialogue** Does your dialogue sound believable when you read it aloud? Are the characters saying things for the sake of the plot, rather than because it seems plausible that they would say them? Is their language appropriate and in keeping with the characters' ages?

- **Ending** Does the ending work? Does it tie up loose ends from the plot, and for the characters? Does the ending feel in keeping with the tone and ideas of the novel? Will the reader be satisfied by the ending?

Focus point

Getting an ending right is a crucial part of writing a satisfying YA novel. Many of the YA novels I receive on submission just suddenly stop, as if the writer abruptly ran out of steam and therefore just stopped writing. That is not satisfying to read. As a writer, you need to always have in the back of your mind where your novel is going, and work hard to give us a conclusion that is worthy of the time we have invested in your narrative.

Write

Write an editorial letter to yourself, answering all of the questions I have highlighted above, as well as others which may occur to you during the reading process. Make sure 1) that you have finished the book and 2) that you have put it away for a month before you try this process. Be honest and critical of your work, and try to get underneath the surface of the novel and question all the decisions you have made.

When I edit a client's book for the first time, I typically write them an editorial letter that addresses the above points systematically. Sometimes, very little needs to be said for several subheadings, but perhaps 'Plot' takes up two pages and 'Character' becomes an essay in and of itself. Often, I pose questions to the writer as I have done above. You need to ask yourself those questions, and be completely honest as you answer them. You also need to honestly ask yourself any questions which occur to you as you read it, for example, 'Why does Johnny fall off his horse at the rodeo when he is actually an excellent rider?' or 'Would Jake kiss Sandra, considering they were fighting for several chapters before that?' Sometimes these questions can be resolved in one or two lines; sometimes these questions will take paragraphs, or whole chapters, to answer. But it is important that you take them seriously and answer them properly. If they do not make sense to you, they will not make sense to your reader.

Key idea

It is important to be able to answer any questions that might come up in the text, and research is a really great way to do this. For example, if you are writing a young adult thriller, and your main character's friend is murdered and she is framed, you need to make sure that the process she goes through with the police feels believable. If your main character has her wisdom teeth removed, the operation should run as a real operation would. If you have doubts about things during the writing process, add in a note to yourself to do the research to answer this issue by the time you come back to the main text.

Once you have written this list addressing the issues in the book, you then need to go back through the manuscript with the list in front of you. At this stage, I recommend using something like 'tracked changes' on your word-processing programme, so that you can see in front of you exactly what you have changed. This can be a really useful tool because often writers will actually think that they have changed far more on the page than they actually have. Sometimes a writer will send me a new draft, but when I look at it, I will see that it is pretty much the same, with only a few sentences changed. Generally speaking, these writers will have answered the question in their head, but not actually transferred that to the page. Obviously, it is important to make sure that the reader, who does not know your characters or world the way you do, can also make sense of the novel.

You will find yourself often doing the following when editing a novel.

CUTTING WORDS

Stephen King once had the advice that you should lose 10 per cent of your word length for your next draft, which is advice he tries to follow even now, as an international bestselling author. It makes a lot of sense. In your first draft you are just trying to get the story down, and you cannot see the wood for the trees. In the next draft, you can focus on making sure that the words on the page are absolutely necessary. Often, you will discover that you were actually 'writing your way in' to a story. I often receive manuscripts where the plot does not kick in until about halfway through the novel. The writer will have their idea, and their characters, but will be spending too long focusing on them, to the detriment of the arc of the story.

ADDING WORDS

You will end up adding a lot of words in a second draft, as well as cutting a lot of words. Some novels will lose 20,000 in a second draft, and gain 20,000 of wholly new material. The word count will remain the same but the actual bulk of the novel will be vastly different. This is something to allow yourself to do. If there are underwritten sections, which require more space in your next draft give them that space. Give your characters time to make big decisions. Let your climactic battle unfold over a chapter rather than being crammed into one or two pages. Allow yourself room to breathe, while also ensuring that you do not allow the pace to lag during the novel.

CUTTING DESCRIPTION

Often, writers over-describe in a first draft. When you look at the manuscript afresh, it should be obvious to you if you have spent too long describing the world, and if the story is getting lost behind the description. If you are struggling with this, go back to the chapter on description, and the chapter on writing rules. Try to apply the adverb and simile exercises to your own novel. Be brave: make those cuts!

Focus point

Sometimes writers are scared of allowing big emotional moments to happen 'on screen', and end up writing them 'off-screen'. This can be easier for the writer, but the reader can end up feeling cheated. Imagine how disappointed you would be if Edward had changed Bella into a vampire 'off the page' in *Twilight*? Or if Lord Voldemort was vanquished 'off the page' in *Harry Potter and the Deathly Hallows*? These emotional moments can be difficult to write, but you owe it to your readership to try to bring them to life on the page.

Addressing structural edits

Once you have written your editorial letter to yourself, it is time to start work on it. At this stage, it is important not to get too bogged down in making small changes, as that can come later. At this stage, you are simply addressing those big overarching issues that have already been flagged in your editorial letter. Setting yourself the task of editing your entire 60,000- or even 100,000-word-long YA novel can seem incredibly overwhelming, however. It is important to try to work through it in stages. Some writers swear by editing a chapter at a time, others go for a whole chunk of the novel.

I am wary of editing chapter by chapter, in separate goes, as I think that this can risk creating a work that is too episodic. But it is definitely necessary to break up the novel somehow, so that you do not feel completely overwhelmed. Try editing your novel in 5,000- to 10,000-word chunks. You will find that some of those chunks do not need much work, and you are only addressing small tweaks here and there in the text. Some of the chunks will require a lot more work, needing whole characters to be rewritten, dialogue to be deleted, or explanations inserted. You might find yourself questioning a lot of what you have written. This is a good thing, and you should never beat yourself up about it. No artist ever sits down at a canvas and expects to paint a masterpiece right away. It is the same with writing. It takes a long time to learn your craft, and you will be learning all the time from what you are doing. You should be proud of that. Maybe the dialogue in the novel is messy, the character motivations don't make sense, and the plot dives off a cliff in the first half. Being aware of that is the first step towards fixing it. Now that you are aware of it, you can try to figure out how to address these issues, rather than turning in a novel which is not good enough – and which is definitely not the best you can do.

It is also a good idea to edit in big chunks, as otherwise you can forget key plot points. If you have a 100,000-word novel and you are editing the final 10,000 words three months after starting the process, you might well find that you have forgotten key plot points or facts about characters. If you build up a consistent and regular editing strategy, you should find it easier to keep track of the characters and plot of your novel.

Key idea

A big part of the editing process is not necessarily about trimming or adding to the words on the page; it is also about the thinking process and time. Don't be afraid to give yourself time to think your way around the issues, rather than staring desperately at your screen trying to get all the problems in your chunk of text solved right away. Go for a walk, away from your computer, and just let your mind wander over the points you are stuck on. Or, if you are lucky enough to have someone in your life who will let you chat about your novel, ask them for input, too. Don't be afraid to come up with bad ideas. After getting the bad ideas out, you can start to focus on the good ones.

Where the story begins

We have looked at whether a story starts too early, but sometimes a story starts too late. Often, writers are panicked about whether their first three chapters are interesting enough to get an agent to call in the full manuscript. What results is a novel that seems to be missing at least one crucial chapter. There is a balance to be struck between throwing us right into the story and giving us too much boring background information. But you need to give the reader time to orient themselves in the world, and time to care about the characters. If you open a novel with Cathy being eaten by a werewolf, it is hard for us to care, as we know nothing about Cathy. If you open a novel with Cathy saving someone else from a werewolf attack, and two chapters in she is eaten by a werewolf, suddenly we care.

Think of how the following films or books would be different if they started in a different place. What if:

- *Titanic* opened with the iceberg hitting?
- *Jurassic Park* began with the dinosaurs escaping?
- *Back to the Future* opened with Marty McFly travelling instantly into the past?

Consider the above examples, and come up with three of your own, from famous books or films. How would they be changed by starting in a different place? What would we gain? What would we lose? Do you think they would still be enjoyable for the reader or viewer?

 ## Snapshot

To get you to think critically about where a story should start, read the following passage and then answer these questions:

- Where does the story start?
- What about the story could be cut?
- Does anything need to be added to the story?

Liza walked into the canteen, head down, hair covering her face protectively. Ever since she had found out that she was descended from the Salem witches, school had been difficult. The other girls in Maybeen's despised the Salem witches as evil troublemakers, and Liza had gone from a nobody to an outcast. She winced as she bumped into a chair. She was still bruised from where Jana had beaten her up earlier in the week, magically flinging book after book at her as she caught up with her in the library. She and Jana had been best friends since they were toddlers, and the emotional bruising was as strong as the physical bruising from this betrayal.

Does the story start in the right place? In my opinion, no. The story definitely starts too late. We are being thrown into a world where there is a magical school, and the Salem witches are real, and Liza has fallen out with her best friend and is being beaten up for her heritage. It makes it hard to care for Liza or her plight, as we know so little about her. Why should we root for her? Is she an evil troublemaker? It also makes it hard to get to grips with this magical world, as we are thrown into it so suddenly. Think about the exercises we have done on establishing world, setting and character.

 ## Write

Have a go at rewriting the above and turning it into your own opening to a YA novel. You can throw out as much of it as you need, and start from scratch, but try to stick to the facts as we know them: that Liza is our main character and that she goes to a magical school. Anything else is up to you. Work hard to create a believable character who we root for, and explain the setting in a way that is not heavy-handed but still allows us to understand the setting of the story better. You still need to work to create a dynamic opening, but one that gives us a chance to understand the world and invest in our main character.

Keep going

Once you have started your structural editing process, it can feel frustrating not to be moving forward with new writing. But you need to remember that if you were to publish or submit the first draft of a story, you would be doing yourself a huge disservice, and you would not be telling the best possible story that you are capable of. My writers, to this day, will find things they want to change even when their books are out there and published and there is nothing they can do about changing them then. You will find that the more time you invest in editing and revising your work, the more you will spot things that you want to change. This is a natural part of the process, and I think it can be an exciting one. You are refining your ideas and creating your best possible work. That is definitely something to be proud of.

Copy-editing

Once you have finished the structural editing process, it is time to get started on the copy-edit.

At this stage, you are focusing more on the smaller issues of the novel. These can involve the following:

- **Continuity errors** Perhaps the character mentions that their star sign is Leo, but later on their birthday is actually in January. Often, characters' ages jump around a lot. Sometimes, characters change names entirely but this isn't picked up on consistently. Make sure that the plot is consistent and that you are not making points which you contradict later on in the novel.

- **Character consistency** Now that you have looked in general at how your characters behave throughout the narrative, look on a more in-depth level at their interactions and actions. Look at the dialogue: would your character say that? Why is she swearing when she says earlier that she hates swearing?
- **Dialogue** Dialogue can be a great tool for adding flow and colour to a novel. But sometimes there is too much dialogue. As well as reading your dialogue aloud, ask yourself:
  - Is it true to the character?
  - Does it further the plot?
  - Does it keep the action moving?
- Sometimes too much dialogue can slow the pace of a novel, and this is something to watch out for.
- **Smaller cuts and additions** As you are reading the novel on a closer level, you will find that there are still a lot of smaller cuts to make. In your structural edit you might have found yourself cutting or moving around big chunks of text. At this stage it is more likely to be deletions of a word or two, a sentence or two, or an occasional paragraph. Consider throughout what each paragraph adds to the story. Does it move the narrative forward? Does it further our understanding of character and setting? If not, why is it there?

Pay attention to small plot points that do not go anywhere. If you mention in great detail that Leah finds her stepfather's air rifle, we will presume that the air rifle has some bearing on the plot. If it never appears again, the reader will be frustrated. This is especially important to bear in mind when you are writing a YA thriller or mystery. Any red herrings need to be deliberate red herrings, and they need to be dealt with at the end. Make sure that everything you set up in the novel goes somewhere.

Look for sentences with too many adjectives or adverbs, and places where there is too much description on its own, making small nips and tucks to the text where necessary.

Snapshot

Take a look at your first chapter. Does it start in the right place? That is, is your novel opening with the most interesting opening it can? Are there any wasted words there, or do you quickly establish your story and characters? Play around with moving around the first paragraphs and deleting the first sentences, in order to see if you are stuck in a style rut and you actually should be starting your story somewhere different.

Bernard Malamud

'I would write a book, or a short story, at least three times – once to understand it, the second time to improve the prose, and a third to compel it to say what it still must say. Somewhere I put it this way: first drafts are for learning what one's fiction wants him to say. Revision works with that knowledge to enlarge and enhance an idea, to reform it. Revision is one of the exquisite pleasures of writing.'

Focus point

Be aware of any favourite words that you might overuse in the novel. Be on the lookout for verbal tics that show up in the text. Often writers will use the same word repeatedly, without even realizing it. Maybe your character sighs a lot, or is always looking shifty. Be on the lookout for too many adverbs, as well. Often, we do not need to know that he moved 'quite' fast, or was 'very' angry: fast and angry are enough on their own.

Proofreading

Now that you have structurally edited and line-edited your novel, it is time to proofread.

This time around, you need to look closely at the following:

- **Spelling** It is a good idea to use a spellchecker on your computer, but make sure that it is switched to the correct form of English (British rather than American).

- **Consistency** If you spell someone's name as Juliana, make sure that it does not become Julianna elsewhere. Ensure that you use either single or double quotation marks throughout. If you italicize internal speech at some points, italicize it throughout the novel.

- **Grammar** Watch for 'its' and 'it's'. Remember to use the correct form of 'there', 'they're' and 'their'. Look out for dialogue, and check that you are closing your dialogue tags and using punctuation correctly.

- **Style** Double-space the manuscript, and use the same font and font size throughout. Arial 10 or Times New Roman 12 are fairly standard. You want your reader to be paying attention to the story rather than getting distracted by different fonts and styles.

Workshop

Look back over the first three chapters of your novel and apply the three stages of editing we have learned in this chapter to your own opening:

Start with a structural edit:

- **Pace:** Does the story have pace throughout?
- **Character:** Do your characters make sense? Will the reader care about the characters and invest in them?
- **World:** Are you giving us enough information to make sense of the setting?
- **Appropriate for YA:** Does the story feel appropriate for your intended audience?
- **Plot:** Have you established your plot within the first three chapters?

- **Style:** Is your style interesting for the reader?
- **Point of view:** Do the voices for your POVs feel authentic and in keeping with the rest of the novel?
- **Dialogue:** Is there too much dialogue, or not enough?

Rework the piece according to your answers to these questions. Then look at the piece on a closer line level, for your copy-edit, paying attention to consistency and continuity. Finally, check your spelling, grammar and style. Read the piece through and compare it to your original piece. Does it feel stronger? Do you feel more confident about it?

Dr Seuss

'So the writer who breeds more words than he needs, is making a chore for the reader who reads.'

Redrafting

Once you have gone through the process once, it is again a good idea to put the novel away for a month (at least) before giving it another pass. The second time around, you might well find that the manuscript feels a lot cleaner. Equally, you might still be discovering issues with the structure and characters. You owe it to yourself not to rush this process. It is important that you put as much time and effort into editing and redrafting as you did into writing that initial draft.

Key idea

When you read the second draft through, you should already be able to see several points where you have improved the manuscript. This helps the – sometimes painful – process feel worth while.

Snapshot

Write down five things about your manuscript that you have improved in the second draft. Take a while to focus on those, and feel positive that you are making your manuscript stronger through this process.

Mark Twain

'The difference between the right word and the nearly right word is the same as the difference between lightning and the lightning bug.'

When do you stop editing?

The reason I recommend finishing the entire novel before you start editing is because sometimes writers can get stuck in an 'editing loop'. This is where you spend so long editing and reworking text that you end up obsessing over the same section, and you never finish the novel. Even once you have finished writing the novel, it is nevertheless possible to get stuck in this loop, doing perhaps 17 or 18 drafts and still not feeling happy with it. Sometimes this is because the novel in its current form is not as strong as it should be, and ultimately you might realize that you need to start working on something else. But sometimes it is not about the manuscript, but just about you being a perfectionist.

My advice is to do a minimum of three drafts (structural editing, copy-editing and proofreading each time), with a minimum of one month between each round of edits. Once you have done at least three drafts, you should think seriously about sending it out to agents or editors. Of course, there are exceptions to this rule and sometimes you will discover that the fourth draft is the one where the magic comes alive. But in general, if your book is going through more than three drafts, you might end up in a stage where you never send it out. Try to give yourself a personal deadline for when you will stop tinkering, and send the manuscript out.

Editing support

Some writers find the editorial process difficult, as they struggle to find the requisite distance from their writing to be as critical as they need to be. Often, people ask me if they need to pay for an editorial report from a professional consultancy prior to submitting. There are some good literary consultancies out there, such as TLC and The Writers' Workshop. However, I would never instruct a writer to spend their hard-earned money on an editorial report. If you have the money, and see it as a worthwhile investment, then do it. But it is absolutely not a necessity.

As a YA writer, SCBWI – or the Society of Children's Book Writers and Illustrators – can be a very helpful resource. By joining SCBWI you get access to their bulletin, podcasts and conferences, which are excellent for networking. Once you join, you also become a member of your local region and through your local chapter you can meet other writers in your locale. There is also a strong online community through their discussion boards. Some writers will post on these boards, or ask their group in person, if anyone is interested in acting as a 'beta reader' for their manuscript. Often it is a two-way process – A reads B's book, and B reads A's book in return. Some people also join 'online critique groups'. These vary from people reading the entire book and commenting, to the author posting up small sections for the whole group to comment on. The Internet is a hugely useful tool for writers now, and it stops the accessibility problem of finding like-minded people in your own town – you can find them online.

Another useful forum is Absolute Write. The Absolute Write forums contain writers from all over the world, writing about topics as diverse as how to find an agent and struggling with characterization. People post reviews of self-publishing companies, ask for help with sticky plot points, and look for advice on their own writing. As the founder, Mac Allister, says: 'We actually *like* you to link your blogs, books, writing-interest sites, and so on. We firmly believe it helps build community, creates stable information environments, improves education, and strengthens relationships.' A lot of writers have found their beta readers or online critique group that way.

If course, if you want to find people to write with in person, there are lots of ways to do this. Some people's local bookshops run a writing group. For example, Big Green Bookshop in London runs two writing groups: a Writing Support Group, to test out your work and get feedback from other writers, and a Critique Group, for those with finished work who are looking to get it published. Your local bookshop, or your local library, might well be able to direct you to a writers' group where you can get help with your editorial work.

 ## Big Green Bookshop Writing Rules

'Rule 1 – Leave your ego at the door. Nobody's work is above constructive criticism.

Rule 2 – Remember you're dealing with people's personal work, thoughts and words. Be constructive, not dismissive.'

Wattpad can also be a helpful way to get feedback on individual chapters, or your story as a whole. By uploading chapters to the site, you can get people to respond to you and give you their comments on your prose.

It is key, however, to remember that not every person will have helpful advice for your work, and you should take it with a pinch of salt. Do not be ego-driven, and never think that your work is perfect, but analyse their comments and assess whether you feel they have worth or not. My advice is take a few days to let the advice settle – the initial feelings of defensiveness can then wear off – and then analyse it to see if it makes sense and has worth. Then try to take it on board. It really is the only way you will improve as a writer.

In this chapter you have learned a lot about how to edit your finished novel, and how to ensure that you make it as polished as it can possibly be. You have analysed plot, characters, worldbuilding and structure, and learned how to distance yourself enough from your words to learn when to cut them. You have learned how to structurally edit your novel and how to copy-edit your novel, and the importance of making sure that every word and every scene are there for a reason.

In the next chapter we will look at sending your completed and edited YA novel out to agents and editors. We will look at how to research agents and editors, how to write a killer query letter and how to write a synopsis; and we will look at the pitfalls of the process. Well done – you have learned a lot so far; it is now time to put this learning into action.

9

Finding an agent

In the last chapter, we looked at editing your novel. You have all of the words down now – hopefully in the right order! – and now it is time to think about getting them out there to a literary agent to find representation. Nowadays, with the advent of self-publishing, there are more paths to publishing than there were before. We will look in-depth at self-publishing, or approaching traditional publishers directly, in later chapters. This book encourages you to think of your writing in a professional sense, and even if you ultimately decide not to look for an agent, understanding their role will help you ensure that this is the right decision for you. However, for a lot of people, a literary agent is still the ultimate goal, and a major step along the way to getting published. In this chapter we will look at what the literary agent does, how to find one, and how to hook one, utilizing a lot of the skills you have developed during the process of writing your young adult novel.

What does an agent do?

An agent is the middleman between an author and a publisher. It is the agent's job to find writers, and then to work with them on editing their book, and then to sell the rights in their book to publishers. It is the agent's job to know the market, negotiate the contracts and make the path to publication – and beyond – as smooth and simple as possible.

Not everyone wants an agent, and not everyone feels that they need one. But nonetheless for many people agents play a crucial role in their writing careers. Most traditional publishers do not accept submissions directly from authors, and will only read submissions through the filter of literary agents. However, the role of the agent goes far beyond simply just getting your book in front of an editor. We will look in more detail at the role of the agent in the process in the next chapter, but this brief overview helps explain their importance.

Agents do the following:

EDIT

Before I submit a book to editors, I edit the book with the client. I typically do a structural edit, asking them those big overarching plot questions, before moving on to a copy-edit, and finally proofreading the piece. Sometimes authors cannot see the wood for the trees when it comes to evaluating their novel. In order for me to take a book on it has to be interesting and marketable, and to feel polished. But there is little to beat that second set of eyes looking at a manuscript and evaluating its strengths as well as its weaknesses. My job is to act like a critical reader, pointing out areas that need work, pointing out logical inconsistencies, or where text needs to be cut or be expanded.

KNOW THE MARKET

It is my job to understand the book market, and to have a keen sense of what sells and what doesn't. It is my job to know whether a particular area of the market is oversaturated, and whether a publisher is investing heavily in a certain kind of book. Remember that, as an author, you will see books just before they come out, at the earliest. I am aware of books are soon as they are sold to publishers, so I can see particular blockbusters or big trends 12–18 months before the the public sees them. It is my job to build relationships with editors and to have a clear sense of their taste, what they are buying and not buying. In each publishing house you might have between one and ten editors commissioning books in the YA genre. I need to know which editor is the best match for which book. For example, I might know that Editor A recently lost out at auction for a big fantasy project for girls, and is looking for something like that, so would be perfect for your book. Or I might know that Editor B has a very full list for the next 18 months and is not currently commissioning any more dystopian novels. It is my job to represent the most saleable works and to find the perfect publisher for them.

NEGOTIATE WITH PUBLISHERS

Contracts with publishers are typically between 15 and 25 pages long, and cover everything from the advance an author is paid, to the royalties, to how they go about getting their rights back if the book goes out of print. It is my job to negotiate every aspect, from who pays for the legal read, to which rights you are granting the publisher, to how much money you will be paid on signature of the contract, and everything in between. Something as small as a percentage increase can make a huge difference to the money that an author sees in the long run.

NEGOTIATE SUBSIDIARY RIGHTS

As well as submitting the book to editors in the primary market I work in – the UK – I also work with co-agents around the world and in different industries in order to secure as many deals as possible for my clients. One of my clients is translated into 32 languages, and it is my job to work with agents in foreign territories who submit the book on my behalf around the world. Most agents will either sell the rights through co-agents abroad, or will have foreign rights agents who sell the rights directly around the world. It is also my job, where possible, to sell film, TV and merchandising rights, with the help of specialist agents in those fields too.

OFFER SUPPORT

Being an author can be incredibly lonely. One of my jobs is to ensure that the author is always happy and informed throughout the process. I give the author business information, explain concepts which they might not understand, read and comment on early ideas and drafts, and support them throughout the process. I act as the middleman between the author and the publisher's editor, so a big part of my job is ensuring that that relationship progresses as smoothly as possible. If the author does not like their book cover, or is late delivering their edits to their publisher, or is not happy with the publicity they are being asked to do, my job is to find a middle route which both sides can be happy with. I am also a big supporter when they have to go out and publicize their book, sitting in the audience of readings, tweeting book reviews, or giving advice before they go onstage. The relationship between author and agent is a close one. Some authors move around several publishers, but typically they will stay represented by one agent throughout their career.

 Agatha Christie

'There was a moment when I changed from an amateur to a professional. I assumed the burden of a profession, which is to write even when you don't want to, don't much like what you're writing, and aren't writing particularly well.'

How to find an agent

The best way to find a list of all agents currently working in the UK is to invest in a copy of *The Writers' and Artists' Yearbook*. Read through that and make a big list of every agency or agent who represents YA fiction. Most agencies will have at least one agent there who represents YA fiction, but make sure that, if they say 'We do not accept YA submissions', you do not put them down on your list, as that would be a rather pointless exercise.

Once you have that list, you need to get online and research those agents. In the past it was difficult to find out anything about agents or agencies. Agents were mysterious beings, in ivory towers, who had little or no interest in unpublished writers.

Nowadays, however, you will find that most – if not all – agencies have a substantial web presence. It is fairly easy to find profiles of agents, their likes and dislikes, a client list, and their submission guidelines. Some agents go above and beyond this and will give interviews online or have their own blogs or Twitter accounts. You need to research every agent or agency on your shortlist online. You might well rule some out at this stage. Perhaps they no longer represent YA, or they only represent fantasy YA, or older YA. Or perhaps they have a very big list of clients already and are no longer looking.

Key idea

Sometimes the younger agent with the smaller list of clients is the best person to submit your book to at an agency. They have more time and inclination to seek out new talent and will be actively looking for clients. Look out for the words 'looking to build my list' – that is the kind of agent you should be submitting your book to, rather than the CEO who is unlikely to have time to look at your work.

Snapshot

Research five agents from your long wish list. Write a profile of each, including at least five clients they represent, what they are particularly eager to represent, and what their submission guidelines are. Write a line about each, explaining why you think your book would be a good fit for them and for their interests.

Submission guidelines

Every agency has similar guidelines, but it is still important to make sure that you are sending them exactly what they ask for. In a world where some agents get 1,000 submissions a month, you do not want to fall at the first hurdle.

Some of the common mistakes I see in submissions are:

- sending me genres I do not represent. I reject those immediately.
- sending me a letter and no sample material. I reject those immediately.
- sending me links to download your material. I reject those immediately.

That probably seems unnecessarily harsh but the reality is that I receive 600 submissions a month and I need to read and respond to those as quickly as possible. If 50 people a month send me a submission with no sample material attached, and I have to respond to each one saying 'Here are my guidelines: please send me three sample chapters', then it eats into time that I could have spent reading submissions by people who have actually done their homework. I never click on links in submissions because you have no way of knowing what you are about to click on. My submission guidelines are laid out clearly in at least three separate places on our company website. If you cannot spare the time to read and follow them, why should I spare the time to read and respond to you? You need to think like a professional, and set your work apart from your competitors'.

 Focus point

Do not make the mistake of presuming that the rules do not apply to you. The rules apply to everyone. Following guidelines makes my life a lot easier, and means that you know from the start that you are setting yourself apart from some of the other people in my inbox.

Most agencies nowadays will accept online submissions rather than physical submissions, but make sure to check this before you start submitting. I only accept online submissions, so whenever I receive a pile of paper in an envelope I am afraid it goes in the bin, unread. At my former agency we only accepted physical submissions, and the process of typing up and signing a letter on headed paper, of trying to find the SAE to send back the material, or weighing and franking and posting... It was a lot of work. As an agent I have a lot of paperwork in my office, and I find online files are much easier to keep track of. I flag a submission when it comes into my inbox, and then I move it into a separate 'Submissions' folder, and tick it off as read once I have responded.

Make sure that you read and write down the submission guidelines of each agency you have researched. At this stage, you should try to create a shortlist of 10–15 agents that you think would be a good fit for your manuscript. Make sure that you note what they are looking for – in submissions, their other clients, and their submission guidelines – in a separate file. When I come to submit manuscripts to editors, I make a spreadsheet of editor name, company, date submitted, and response. I advise all writers to do the same. It allows you to ensure that you have sent to the right people, that you don't send to the same person more than once, and allows you to keep track of where you are in the process.

Snapshot

Make a spreadsheet of the ten-plus literary agents you want to submit your manuscript to. Include their name, company, and what their submission guidelines are in your spreadsheet. Putting it down on paper will help make this feel a more concrete step towards your goal of getting published.

Key idea

Some people will tell you to send to only one agent at a time, but I think that this is a bad idea. It can take some agents three months to respond, and you would spend several years sending your manuscript out on this basis. A better method, in my opinion, is to send it out to batches of five to eight agents at a time. Some of those first five might have useful feedback, and if they do you can then edit the manuscript before sending it out to the next five.

The submission package

What most agents ask for in submissions is a cover letter, a synopsis, and the first three chapters (or approximately the first 50 pages) of the book. It is important to get this stage right, but not to obsess over every tiny detail. For example, no one ever got rejected because they used Arial rather than Times New Roman. Treat this like you would a professional application for a job and you will be on the right lines.

The cover letter

In the cover letter, you are aiming to introduce your manuscript in a way that whets the agent's appetite, and briefly introduce yourself, as well as giving them any extra information they might need to have.

Key idea

Your cover letter for your YA novel should be 90 per cent about your book and 10 per cent about you – not the other way around.

For the sake of this chapter, I want you to imagine that I have written a YA novel entitled *Cross My Heart*. I will now talk you through how I would go about submitting *Cross My Heart* to literary agents:

Dear Ms Agent,

Please find attached the synopsis and first three chapters of my YA thriller *Cross My Heart*, which is complete at 75,000 words. *Cross My Heart* follows 16-year-old Lexi's search for her missing best friend in their English seaside village, forcing her to uncover and confront the secrets at the heart of their relationship.

[This is just a very simple paragraph introducing what you are attaching and showing that you are following the submission guidelines. Showing an awareness of genre, word count, and introducing very briefly your novel's themes is a great way to show me that you are taking this seriously.]

Lexi and Abbie have done everything together their whole lives. First school, first kiss, first love: the lot. So when Abbie goes missing, the day after her sixteenth birthday, Lexi's world is plunged into turmoil. Abbie's parents think she has run away, but Lexi knows that Abbie would never leave her behind: they both had ambitions that reached far beyond their sleepy village. In the weeks after the disappearance their tiny community becomes a hotbed of gossip and rumour, but if anyone knows anything, they are not telling. Because Abbie had a secret. A big secret. And maybe, just maybe, someone would kill to keep her quiet.

[This paragraph is a blurb. It is not designed to give away the ending of the novel, or to reveal too much information behind it. It is designed, instead, to intrigue the reader. You need to give away some information in your blurb: setting, character, conflict. But you should not get too bogged down by introducing all your characters and every plot twist and turn. You want to establish tension, and introduce the main conflict at the heart of the novel so that the agent is intrigued and wants to read more.]

Cross My Heart is an atmospheric teen thriller, full of twists and turns, but at its heart it is about growing up, first friendship, and the lies we tell those who love us the most. *Cross My Heart* would sit alongside other YA thrillers such as *Heart Shaped Bruise* by Tanya Byrne, *Girl, Missing* by Sophie McKenzie and *How to Fall* by Jane Casey. I have ideas for future novels in a similar vein, and my next novel will be about a murder at an elite Sussex boarding school.

[*This paragraph shows that you have considered your market and researched where your book would sit. You do not need to know precisely where your book would sit, but you need to have a rough idea of which books other readers would like as well as your book. Try to be focused when considering titles, and try to include at least one comparison title. I have also mentioned that I plan to write more books in this genre. Agents will often want to know what you do next so it is worth mentioning a future idea here.*]

My name is Juliet Mushens, I am in my late twenties, and I live in London, where I work in publishing. I am a passionate YA reader and have had a macabre interest in crime fiction my entire life. You can find me on twitter at @mushenska.

[*This paragraph needs to contain just a few lines about you. You don't need to include your age, but it is a chance for the agent to get to know a little bit more about you. If you have any writing credits such as short stories, competition wins, or previous novels, feel free to mention them here. Equally, if you don't, then just keep it short and punchy.*]

I hope you enjoy reading the chapters as much as I enjoyed writing them, and I look forward to hearing from you.

Yours sincerely,

Juliet Mushens.

[*My ending is professional and to the point. It is not over-familiar or pushy. If the agent wants more, they will ask for more. All you can do now is wait.*]

Snapshot

Revisit our earlier exercise of summing up your own novel in a sentence. Remember that if you are struggling with this, a simple way is to focus on CHARACTER, in SETTING, experiences CONFLICT to achieve RESOLUTION. In my example, 16-year-old Lexi (CHARACTER), in a seaside village (SETTING) loses her best friend (CONFLICT) and must find her (RESOLUTION). The key thing you need to do in this short pitch is to establish the conflict, because that will tell the agent what the book is about and make them keen to read on.

Writing a blurb

Writing a blurb for your book can seem really difficult at first. You are very close to the work, after all, and it can be incredibly difficult to tell people what your work is about without feeling the need to tell them every aspect of plot and character. However, a blurb is entirely different from a synopsis in that you only need to focus on the main arc, rather than on telling us every small detail of the book.

In our previous exercise you had to come up with an elevator pitch: a snappy sentence which sums up what your work is about.

We talked about

- CHARACTER
- SETTING
- CONFLICT.

Once you have your two-sentence pitch, it can be a lot easier to extend that into a more detailed blurb. A blurb should be a minimum of one paragraph and can be as detailed as two. However, try to make sure that you do not end up telling too much about the book. You want to hold back the twists and turns of your plot so that the agent wants to read more.

Have a go at doing so, using the following prompts:

Snapshot

Write your own blurb for the two prompts below:

CHARACTER – 14-year-old Daniel

SETTING – The Tower of London in the 1500s

CONFLICT – Daniel is asked to spy on the Tower's prisoners for Henry VIII, but is secretly Catholic

CHARACTER – 15-year-old Maria

SETTING – a medieval fantasy world

CONFLICT – the prince goes missing and Maria finds him: he reveals a conspiracy to destroy the kingdom

Now give it a go for your own work. Try to create suspense and excitement for the reader.

By expanding on these lines, you can easily build up a more detailed picture of your novel.

Focus point

Get into the habit of reading the blurbs on the back of published books and looking online at descriptions for books. Which make you want to read on? Which do you end up putting back? You need to create intrigue and tension within your blurb, hinting at mysteries to come that the agent will want to read to find out about.

Here are some example blurbs from cover letters for books that I have represented and sold:

THE MINIATURIST by Jessie Burton

I was hoping that you would read the first three chapters of my novel *The Miniaturist*.

It tells the story of a wealthy, dysfunctional family living in Amsterdam in 1686 during the decline of the Dutch Golden Age. Set against the backdrop of the Calvinist church, the gossip of guilds and the overblown trading of the Dutch East India Company, it explores the tyranny and safety of home and the need for secrets and imagination, all linked by a mysterious miniaturist existing on the edge of their lives.

When the merchant Johannes Brandt commissions a miniature version of his wife's new marital home to be built, its construction under the influence of the elusive miniaturist unleashes long-suppressed secrets, lost love, old wounds and hidden hopes. All the inhabitants are forced to look into their souls and one another's hearts and decide whether they have the strength to carry on in a society which might end up condemning them all.

THE OATHBREAKER'S SHADOW by Amy McCulloch

For fifteen years Raim has worn a single blue string tied in an intricate knot around his wrist. Raim barely thinks about it at all; not since becoming the most promising young archer ever to train for the elite Yun guard and not since his best friend (and the future Khan) Khareh asked him to become his sole Protector. But on the most important day of his life, when he binds his life to Khareh's, suddenly that string on his wrist is all he can think about – it bursts into flames and sears a dark mark into his skin. The knot contained a promise of its own – and now that promise is broken.

Scarred now as an oathbreaker, Raim has two options: run, or be killed.

Raim flees deep into the vast desert to live in Lazar: the colony of exiled oathbreakers. It is there he hopes to learn how to clear his name and return home to keep his promise to Khareh. Except in Lazar, he discovers that his scar from the burnt thread marks the first step on the path to becoming a sage, with the ability to perform feats of magic straight out of legend. The trade-off: he will remain tarnished as an oathbreaker for the rest of his life. Can he forgo his honour for immense power? And even if he did want to clear his name, how can he keep a promise he never even knew he made in the first place?

THE BLACKHEART LEGACY by Liz de Jager

Thank you so much for being kind and agreeing to look at the first three chapters of my YA manuscript: *Grimm Tales: The Blackhart Legacy*, complete at 72,200 words.

Kit Blackhart, has a lot on her plate, and it's not just staying alive while fighting monsters either. She's keen to prove herself worthy of being a Blackhart, but when she's tossed into a situation where she has to deal with the fae realm being overthrown and a young prince needing her help, she realizes that her past year's combat training and tedious Latin lessons will only help her that much. Forced to rely on new friends, Kit has to save herself, the handsome fae prince and, above all, both his world and ours from complete destruction at the hands of a fanatical acolyte of the Elder Gods.

The Blackhart Legacy will suit fans of Sarah Reese Brennan's *Demon Lexicon* books and Melissa Marr's *Wicked Lovely* novels.

 Julie Andrews

'Perseverance is failing 19 times and succeeding the 20th.'

 Key idea

The best cover letters are short and punchy, and give the agent enough information to whet their appetite, but not enough to make them bored. Try to aim for one A4 page, double-spaced. Keep refining your letter until you get there.

Write

Utilizing what you have learned from the example submission letters, and the exercises in writing an elevator pitch and a blurb, have a go at writing your own cover letter for the novel you are working on. Think about word count, genre, and where it sits in the market. Address it to a particular agent you have chosen from your list and make sure that you give them all the information they have requested.

The synopsis

Most agents request a synopsis with your novel. Often, when I submit a book to an editor, they will also request a synopsis for future books in the series, so it is a good idea to have those planned out. I ask for a synopsis with the first three chapters of a novel for several reasons:

- It shows that the author has planned and plotted out the entire novel, and hopefully shows that they have written it, too.
- It helps me see whether they are in control of their plot and that the novel has a strong narrative arc.
- I can see where the novel ends, and if the novel feels in keeping with the sample chapters.

Sometimes, a synopsis can help me see obvious problems within a book. A novel might start as a compelling contemporary romance but when I read the synopsis it becomes clear that very little actually happens in the story. A synopsis can also highlight gaps or logical inconsistencies in the plot. And finally, it can also show me whether the book has a strong ending. Some books sound great and then the synopsis shows that they wake up and discover that it was all a dream, or a hallucination. Synopses help me identify these problems early on.

However, try not to get too hung up on writing a perfect synopsis. It is next to impossible to write one that is interesting and stimulating. I can see that your writing is interesting and stimulating from the sample chapters – so think of the synopsis as a technical document outlining the backbone of the plot.

A synopsis is very different from a blurb. A blurb is a selling document, designed to get the reader interested and intrigued enough to want to read the book itself. A synopsis is a technical document. A blurb tells you about mysteries and hints at twists and turns, but it is the synopsis that will tell you who dies at the end.

Writing your elevator pitch and your blurb will be really helpful tools to get you to see your work in a commercial light, and for you to consider how to present it to a literary agent or publishing company. You should aim for your synopsis to be no more than two A4 pages. If an agent wants to see a chapter-by-chapter breakdown, they will specifically ask to see that, but the majority of agencies just want a general synopsis.

In your synopsis you should be expanding on the elements that we looked at in your pitch:

- CHARACTER
- SETTING
- CONFLICT.

You also need to show the reader the **conclusion** of the novel. In a blurb you can hint at the conclusion, but in a synopsis you need to lay it out more clearly.

The planning document you put together when writing your novel comes in very useful when it is synopsis time.

You need to lay out:

- the set-up of the novel

This is how it starts.

- the inciting incident

What is it that kicks the plot into high gear?

- the second act

Lay out how the protagonist attempts to resolve the conflict.

- the third act

This resolves the story and its subplots. Explain the climax of the novel here, too.

We have already looked at the character arc and the wider arc. You need to tie in your character arc to the wider arc of the novel in your synopsis, explaining the changes that your protagonist goes through.

Key idea

Sometimes the reason you find writing a synopsis difficult is because you have an overly complicated plot. If you are really struggling to write it, it could be because there are issues within the structure of the novel itself, which you need to go back and address.

THINGS TO WATCH OUT FOR

- **Length** Do not let your synopsis extend for more than two pages. It makes the reader think that you have an unwieldy plot.
- **Style** The synopsis should be written in third-person present tense. Do not be tempted to try to write it in a different style so that it 'stands out'. Let it do the job it is intended to do.
- **Subplots** You do not need to detail every single subplot when writing the synopsis. You can focus on the main arc, and the key subplots that tie into and further the plot.

Stanley Ellin

'No one put a gun to your head and ordered you to become a writer. One writes out of his own choice and must be prepared to take the rough spots along the road with a certain equanimity, though allowed some grinding of the teeth.'

A SYNOPSIS EXAMPLE

Using the example of my made-up YA novel, *Cross My Heart*, I will lay out a synopsis for it, highlighting useful points for you to take on board when you are drafting your own.

Cross My Heart opens on the day of Abbie Jones's sixteenth birthday party. Lexi is Abbie's best friend and confidante. The girls dream of escaping their claustrophobic home town of Swanage, in Dorset, and going to university in London. Their parents are critical of their hopes, so they rely on one another, as well as leaning on their charismatic form tutor Mr Watkins.

The day after the party Abbie disappears, leaving behind a worried Lexi. The police are called and begin to investigate, but it seems to them to be a clear-cut case of a teenager running away. When a letter arrives, purporting to be from Abbie, claiming that she is in London now and will not be coming back until after the summer, the case is closed. The gossip at school dies down and everyone starts to move on. Everyone but Lexi.

Lexi receives a note in her locker from the class misfit, Daniel, who tells her that Abbie had secretly been working for his online business. She had been saving up for university, and he does not believe that she would abandon her plans for her future. With Daniel on her side, Lexi starts to investigate further.

Lexi's parents are fed up with her obsession. They make her face some home truths about how she lived in Abbie's shadow, as well as seeing the possibility that maybe Abbie did just leave her behind. Lexi talks to her schoolteacher, Mr Watkins, and is upset when he echoes her parents' words and tells her to leave it alone.

Daniel manages to get access to Abbie's emails and discovers that she was secretly emailing a man named Mr X, and arranging to run away with him. Mr Watkins asks Lexi to meet him after school, so he can apologize, and tell her that he knows more about the disappearance than she thought.

Mr Watkins reveals that Abbie was having an affair with the head teacher at the school, and that she ran away when their relationship ended. Lexi refuses to believe him and they argue on the cliffs in front of the beach. He pushes her into the water – knowing how dangerous the tide is – and leaves her there. No one knows where she has gone, so no one will look for her.

Lexi manages to swim back to shore, with the help of Daniel. He tells her that he is sure that Mr Watkins is Mr X and that he has led Abbie to believe that he will come for her once the attention has died down. But Daniel suspects that he is grooming other girls in the school.

Lexi confronts Mr Watkins at his house, as Daniel secretly films him. He reveals that Abbie is in London, waiting for him, but that he never cared for her. He tells Lexi that if she doesn't leave him alone he will 'get rid of her'. The police turn up, and Mr Watkins is taken into custody. Daniel and Lexi finally give into their feelings and kiss.

The case causes a huge scandal and Abbie finally returns home. Lexi has changed in her absence. She now no longer needs Abbie, although she does still want to be friends. The girls confront the truths of their own relationship and decide to move on. Daniel and Lexi become a couple. Mr Watkins goes to prison.

As you can see, this synopsis deals with the main narrative arc but also talks about the character arc. There might be several subplots in the novel that are not mentioned here: this is because the synopsis is designed to be the backbone of the novel, rather than focusing on every single thing that happens. This synopsis deals with SETTING, CHARACTER, CONFLICT and CONCLUSION. It introduces us to the main characters, the inciting incident, details the escalation of the plot, and talks us through the conclusion and aftermath.

Write

Using the guidance above and my example synopsis, have a go at writing your own synopsis. Once you are done, ask a friend who has not read your work to read it through – ask them whether it makes sense to them. Sometimes, we do not put information on the page because we assume that it is apparent to our audience, but this is not always the case. Make sure that the story makes sense for a layperson coming to it fresh.

C.S. Lewis

'Failures are finger posts on the road to achievement.'

The first three chapters

As well as a cover letter and synopsis, most agents ask for the first three chapters, or approximately 50 pages of your novel. We will not spend too much time on this, as you should have already edited your manuscript to within an inch of its life. What you need to ensure, however, is that your first 50 pages are interesting enough to capture and keep an agent's attention. You need to strike a balance between throwing too much action and plot information at us, and starting a novel far too slowly.

Once you have your submissions package together, it is important to put it away for a week and then look at it with fresh eyes. Spelling errors, typos and issues within the writing are much more likely to become apparent to you once you have a bit more distance from the novel itself.

Focus point

If you find yourself telling readers 'it really gets going in Chapter 4!' ask yourself why you aren't starting the novel in Chapter 4.

Edit

Give your first three chapters one more editorial pass, keeping in mind that you are doing your utmost to capture the agent's attention from the start. That isn't to say that you need to open the novel with an explosion or a murder, but you do need to consider carefully whether you are starting the novel in the right place.

Social media and promoting yourself

Many people get hung up on their 'social media presence' and how to promote themselves, believing that they need to have thousands of Twitter followers, a Facebook page and a blog, in order to even be considered by a literary agent. The reality is that it will ultimately come down to the quality of your manuscript. I have signed people who have no Twitter followers, and rejected people with 40,000 Twitter followers. What is important to me, and to many literary agents, is that you do not have a negative online presence. If I Google your name, what will come up? Will it be a Twitter where you spend your time cursing your neighbours, your children's teacher and your husband? Will it be an Instagram full of inappropriate photographs? Will it be a blog where you talk about 'horrible agents' and 'hateful editors'? You need to look at your online presence and make sure that it is a positive expansion of the message of your books. You also need to make sure that you do not over-promote yourself. Unless you are invited by agents to send them Twitter pitches, through online pitching competitions such as PitchMas and QueryKombat, make sure that you keep your interactions with agents appropriate and professional.

I probably won't remember everyone who interacts with me on Twitter, but if someone uses Twitter to spam me with links to their book, or is rude to me, then you can guarantee that I won't want to represent him/her. If you do interact with professionals, do not constantly send them links to your book, or ask them inappropriate questions. While not having social media is not a bad thing, having social media and using it negatively certainly is a bad thing.

Jennifer Laughran, literary agent

'Social media of all kinds, including/especially Twitter, is all about … well, being SOCIAL. It's about connecting with people on a human level – not about YOUR BOOK YOUR BOOK YOUR BOOK.'

Workshop

Look again at your cover letter and ask yourself the following questions:

- Does it contain the information that the agent has asked for?
- Are your spelling and grammar impeccable?
- Do you mention the salient points of genre, word count and age range?
- Are there at least two comparative titles mentioned?
- Is your blurb intriguing, rather than confusing?
- Is the letter 90 per cent about the book and 10 per cent about you?
- Does the letter encourage you to turn to the chapters?

If there is anything missing, you need to go back and turn to your letter again, taking inspiration from the example blurbs included in this chapter, as well as my suggested guideline letter.

Next step

In this chapter we have looked at why you might want an agent. We have also looked at how to research the right agent for you, and how to put together your submission package for the agent of cover letter, synopsis and first three chapters. We have looked at what makes a good cover letter, how to craft a synopsis, and whether or not your novel starts in the right place.

In the next chapter we are going to look at traditional publishing and self-publishing models, so you can make sure that you pick the method right for you.

10

Different types of publishing: self and traditional

In the last chapter we looked at putting together a submissions package for an agent. In this chapter, we are going to look in more depth at what a traditional agent and publishing deal can offer you. However, the face of publishing has changed a lot in recent years, and we are also going to look at what self-publishing can offer, and how to analyse whether or not it is right for you. As with all things regarding your novel, you owe it to yourself to put in the time and effort to properly research how you want your book to be published. In this chapter you will get a clearer idea of what you can expect from traditional publishing, and from self-publishing, and have a better sense of which will be right for you, and for your book.

Literary agents and thinking professionally

The majority of traditional publishers will not consider a work unless it is submitted to them by a literary agent. This is not true of all publishers, and we will look at that later in this chapter, but the vast majority of traditional presses will only read works when an agent has been the one to send it to them. This is because the agent acts as an initial filter for submissions, and is only showing them the best projects. This is also because a lot of publishers prefer to deal with an agent, who understands the business side of publishing. An agent is used to negotiating, and understands the industry, and can make the process run more smoothly for the publisher as well as for the author!

Agents are not paid by the author – and if any agent ever asks you for fees to sign with them, you should run in the opposite direction. The agent, however, does take a percentage of the advance and royalties. The typical structure is 15 per cent for a deal in the agent's home market, 20 per cent for overseas deals and 20 per cent for film rights. These percentages are very standard, and you should question your agent if they offer other percentages. I once had a writer offer me 40 per cent commission if I would take on their book! This also means that the agent has a real impetus to work very hard for you as they make no money unless they are making you money.

But what happens once you have a literary agent? What does the process look like once you have a book on submission?

Firstly, you should expect to do some more editorial work on your novel with the literary agent. Some agents do not do editorial work, but more and more, as the market for debuts becomes increasingly competitive, agents will undertake rigorous editing with a client. Typically, when I sign someone, I expect the book to go through a structural edit and a copy-edit, and then be proofread.

I am always upfront about my edits when signing a client, as there is little point agreeing to work with someone if you have different views about where the novel is going, or the kind of author the author wants to be in the future. The agent will normally lay out their suggested edits for your book in a phone call, meeting, or in an editorial letter, and it is then up to you to take them on board and work on the novel again. Sometimes, having that professional guidance there is what it takes to unlock the potential from within your manuscript.

I often ask authors to consider the following questions when we start working together:

- How do you see your books being packaged and marketed?
- Which other authors do you think are comparable to your writing?
- Where would you like to see your career in ten years' time?

Snapshot

Answer these questions about your own work. Focus on how you would like to see your book pitched and sold in an ideal world, and look at the careers of other authors you admire and who seem to be writing in the same genre as you are.

Write

Write a statement of intent about your own career and writing. Set yourself goals for where you will be in six months, one year, two years and five years. Have objectives that are SMART: specific, measurable, achievable, timely and realistic. A smart goal would be: 'In six months I will be halfway through the first draft of my novel' or 'In one year I will be editing a draft of my finished novel.' Visualizing these goals can really help focus your mind on where you want to be in the future.

These questions help both of us establish whether we are on the same page with regard to the book. For example, if an author sees their YA novel as very literary and wants it to become a prize-winner, and I think that it is a very commercial project that will appeal to YA romance fans, then it becomes clear that we have a problem. However, most times, when I meet an author, we end up agreeing in general with where we see the book going. I have a thorough understanding of the YA market, as do all YA agents, and we can help the author avoid common pitfalls and issues in order to find their book a home with a good publisher.

The editing process is normally a lot of fun. My authors are often surprised at how enjoyable it can be once you have another pair of eyes casting over the work! Rather than just you looking at your novel over and over again – and reaching a point where you cannot see the wood for the trees – an agent will provide a fresh viewpoint on your work. Often there will be issues which you know are there, but are stumped as to how to fix, and the agent can point them out and bat ideas around with you until you find a point where both of you are happy. Sometimes the changes an agent suggests are radical – losing a character, for example, or changing viewpoint. But often the author will discover, while doing these edits, that actually making these changes frees them from issues within the book and creates a much more satisfying storyline as a result.

Once the author has done big edits, I then look at the book on a line-by-line level, picking out issues and problems that are smaller within the text. Sometimes undergoing the big structural changes can get rid of these; sometimes, however, it means that a character who no longer exists is referred to a couple of times, or a plot point which was deleted is still appearing in a few places. The line edit picks up these continuity issues, but it also might pick up points where the pace lags or the dialogue does not ring true. Once these changes have been made, the book will be proofread, to try to pick up any stray errors. It will be formatted and made to look as professional as possible – page numbers and a header detailing author name and title are a must, as well as the agent's contact details on the cover page. Then it is ready to go.

 Focus point

Editing is a dialogue, not a monologue. You are well within your rights to disagree with some edits, but you should try to be as objective as possible and take on board your agent's comments. You are on the same team with the same goal: to get you a publishing deal and start off an exciting writing career.

Preparing for submission

Once you have done your edits with an agent, the agent will start submitting your book to publishers. A key part of the agent's job is to build relationships with editors at publishing houses in the market they work in. It is my job to know which areas each editor is looking to buy in, which we discussed briefly in the last chapter. Within each publishing house there will be several imprints. For example, Puffin is an imprint of Penguin Random House, and Orchard is an imprint of Hachette publishers. Within each imprint there will be between two and eight commissioning editors, i.e. editors with the power to buy novels from agents. Each editor will have a different remit and taste, and it is the agent's job to understand that implicitly, and to tailor a submission to the person who is most likely to buy the book.

Jennifer Laughran, literary agent

'Some [authors] want to know what's up more often, and that's fine. And some authors REALLY REALLY want to know every gory detail as it happens – that's fine too, they can just let me know. I happen to think it is a bit unhealthy for the majority of authors, but of course I will send as my author prefers.'

As well as the fact that most publishers only look at submissions through an agent, it is also worth considering that the agent has the insider knowledge to know which editor is best for a particular project. There is no point sending a gritty YA urban fantasy to an editor who specializes in middle-grade romance, for example. I have to know which editor in each imprint is most likely to want to look at the book I am submitting. I also look at which books that editor has bought recently. They might have bought a YA Western, so I would not choose to send one to them. But perhaps they were the under-bidder for a YA Western, in which case they might be more eager to buy that particular novel from me.

Pitching to editors

I build up my list of editors to submit to, and then I call them to pitch the book to them.

I always let my clients know the editor's name, publishing house, and date I am submitting the novel. I will let the editor know how many books I am offering, when I want to hear back from them by, and pertinent information about the author. I send them my own equivalent of the cover letter the author sends to agents, so I know first-hand how tough they can be to write!

Key idea

Before I send an editor a client manuscript, I always call them first to pitch it to them. Over the phone I give some brief information, an elevator pitch, and explain why I am excited about the book. It is a great way to make sure I know everything about a manuscript and project, as I am having to talk about it to the interested party.

Snapshot

Look again at the elevator pitch you wrote earlier, and try reading it to other people to see what they think. Then put the elevator pitch away and try telling people about it without anything written down to prompt you. Ask them to ask you a few questions about it. Give yourself five minutes maximum for this conversation, and ask them afterwards for their feedback on your pitching.

Once I have pitched on the phone, I send them a pitch letter. Below, you can see an example of a pitch for the novel *The Fire Sermon* by Francesca Haig. It was first published in February 2015, and will be published in 26 languages, with Dreamworks optioning for film rights.

Dear [editor name],

As discussed, I am incredibly excited to attach *The Fire Sermon* by Francesca Haig. This is a high-concept YA/crossover novel that combines the literary sensibilities of novels such as *Never Let Me Go* and *The Road* with the character-driven, high-concept action of *The Hunger Games* and *Noughts and Crosses*. Francesca was a slush-pile author and was offered representation by three other agents: I was determined to sign her as I found the book both incredibly compelling and beautifully written.

Four hundred years after a nuclear apocalypse, in a society without technology, all humans are twins. One of each pair is an Alpha, physically perfect, while the other is an Omega, bearing some form of mutation. In the apartheid-like society, Omegas are branded and forced out to settlements on blighted land. But although they live apart, they die together; when one dies, it kills the other.

Cass is one of the rare Omegas whose mutation isn't visible: she is a seer, plagued by glimpses of the future, and by repeated visions of a mysterious island where an Omega resistance is growing. From early childhood she learns to disguise her difference, delaying the moment when she will be branded and sent away from her family. Unsplit, she and her twin, Zach, can't assume their allotted roles in society, and so grow up isolated, intertwined by both closeness and resentment, until her 'gift' is finally revealed. Branded and sent away, she ekes out an existence at an Omega settlement, where over the next few years she hears rumours of Zach's rise to the ruling Alpha council.

When she is seventeen, Zach has her abducted and imprisoned to ensure his safety. After two years of imprisonment, Cass escapes, and uncovers her brother's plans to ensure a world where Omegas can no longer be used against their Alpha counterparts. Cass heads for the fabled island to join the Omega resistance, but is she alone in her idealism that they can live peacefully side by side with the twins? And what will they do when they learn who her brother is?

The Fire Sermon works as a standalone but Francesca has plotted out the remaining two books in the trilogy.

Francesca Haig is in her 30s and lives in London with her husband. She achieved her PhD at the University of Melbourne and is a Senior Lecturer at the University of Chester, where she is also Programme

Leader in Creative Writing. Her poetry and prose has been published in many literary journals and anthologies in both Australia and the UK, and has won various prizes. In 2010 she was awarded a Hawthornden Fellowship. *The Fire Sermon* is her first novel.

I am offering UK & Commonwealth rights (excluding Canada and excluding audio) for the trilogy, and would like an indication of interest as soon as possible. I am simultaneously submitting this in the US and in translation.

This is an incredible debut, which provokes many questions that will resonate with teens and adults alike. When is a freedom fighter a terrorist? Does society always need a scapegoat? Can killing one person to save the lives of many ever be a moral choice?

I hope you feel as passionately about *The Fire Sermon* as I do and look forward to hearing from you shortly.

All best,

Juliet

Focus point

A lot goes on behind the scenes when an agent is preparing to submit a manuscript. They work hard to ensure that they are sending the project to the right editors, in order to secure the author a good deal.

Selling the rights

One of the key things the agent does before submitting a manuscript is distinguish which rights they are willing to sell. I will break down here the common territories that are sold to publishers and the pros and cons of each.

UK AND COMMONWEALTH

Most UK agents will sell only UK and Commonwealth rights, excluding Canada. This gives the publisher the rights to publish the book in the English language, and to ship this version as an export copy into British Commonwealth countries. This then allows the agent the opportunity to do separate deals for the book in other languages, and in other countries. It gives the agent more control over the book, and gives them and the author more control over which publishers overseas they sell the book to.

WORLD ENGLISH

This grants the publisher the right to publish the book in the English language throughout the world. This means that the publisher can either sell on the rights to the book to an American publisher (keeping a percentage of the advance for themselves), or that they can get their sister company to publish the book as a co-edition, and pay the author a royalty on each copy sold. The pros of this can be the author gets more money upfront, and that it might then be more likely that the publisher will get a US deal as the publisher can put pressure on their sister company to publish the book in the US. The cons are that the publisher takes a cut of the money, and that sometimes other publishing companies are reluctant to buy rights from a publisher that is not part of their corporation.

WORLD ALL LANGUAGES

This grants the publisher the right to publish the book in all languages throughout the world. This means that the publisher can sell the book in any number of translated languages, as well as into the American market. The pros of this are that the author might get a much bigger advance, and some rights teams are very proactive in selling rights around the world. The cons are a lack of control, and that the publisher takes a percentage of the income from each deal that is struck.

I prefer, where possible, to do only UK deals. I then use co-agents around the world – agents working in foreign territories – to handle and sell my books in other countries. This means that I can be more agile, move fast where necessary and – unlike a publisher's rights teams – I am not trying to sell rights in 100+ books. I have a small and select list, which means that I can be much more responsive to quick movement. Foreign income can also make a huge difference to an author. I have one children's author whose UK deals amount to five figures, but who makes six figures from the other countries who publish his books around the world. Some of my authors will be published in 30-plus languages around the world, which is a huge source of revenue for them. Numerous rights deals can make publishers very excited about a debut, as it hints that it will go on to sell well, if it achieves this level of enthusiasm all around the world.

Types of deal

There are also different types of deal that publishers make. Deals may be pre-emptive or made through running an auction.

PRE-EMPT

A pre-emptive deal is when a publisher moves very quickly to offer on a book. Normally, they will offer a lot of money, but want more rights than the agent is offering, in order to take the book off the table. It is the agent's job to weigh up whether this is the right editor, right company, and right offer, or whether the author might get more money in the long run if the book went to auction.

AUCTION

If you have established that more than one publisher wants to bid for the rights to a book, then you will run an auction. Auctions can hugely inflate the amount of money your book goes for, and can also encourage publishers around the world to offer, as a book is creating a big buzz.

Once you have established that more than one publisher is bidding, the agent will email all of the editors the rules: the rights that are being offered, and in how many books. They then give them a deadline for when they want the offer by. Once the offers are all in, you call all editors, tell them where they came in the auction pecking order, tell them the highest bid, and ask them if they want to bid again.

Say in round one you had four publishers bidding. A bid 10,000, B bid 7,000, C bid 12,000 and D bid 20,000. You would call B, then A, then C, then D, and ask them whether they want to bid again. The publishers would have to top the previous highest-round bid in order to continue to the next round. Sometimes the money can increase thirty-fold during an auction. The final round of the auction is known as 'best bids', whereupon the editors put forward their best and biggest royalties and advance. Sometimes they commit to marketing and publicity plans at the same time. I always reserve the right not to go with the highest bidder, and will normally try to get the author to meet the publishers before we do final bids. Sometimes the author will like a certain publisher best, and even if the money is lower, they will still want to go with them.

The key thing to remember is that the agent is working for the author, and advising them to make the best decision for their long-term career. The agent provides expertise and support. The agent also provides distance from the process.

One of my clients negotiated his first book deal directly with the publisher. He struggled when negotiating the deal because it can be a combative process – the publisher is out to make the best deal for them, and the author does not necessarily have enough experience to counter what they are offering. The author also feels a personal connection to the book – of course – and just wants to sign a deal without appearing 'difficult'. The role of the agent is to go into bat for the author, and ensure that they are receiving the best royalties and best advance. The devil is in the detail with contracts and the agent has a wealth of experience to draw on when negotiating them. The story of my client has a happy ending: when I did the next deal for my client, the royalties were vastly improved, and the advance was ten times as much as he had got for the first deal.

Write

Have a go at writing your own pitch letter to an editor, as if you are selling them your novel from the perspective of an agent. You need to include the following information:

- How many books are you selling?
- What genre is the book in?
- Can you think of comparison titles?
- Which rights are you selling?
- What relevant information about the author do you need to share with them?

Keep this cover letter to a maximum of one A4 page. Try to distance yourself from the book as a writer, and view it in the way an editor and publisher would. What is the key information to convey, and why?

Susan Hawk, literary agent

'The best way to make sure that your book is aligned to the market is to read, read, read. Read as widely as you can in the category you're writing.'

Key idea

The agent provides a barrier between the author and the business side of publishing. While the agent should tell you every detail that transpires, it is their job to protect you from difficult conversations, and to work hard to achieve the best deal possible for the author.

The publishing process

Once a book has been accepted by a publisher, the next step is the editorial process. I said in the chapter on editing that it was important to try to enjoy the editorial process, and part of that is because there will be a lot of editing in your career! The editor at your publisher will typically again do a structural edit, then a line-edit, then you will have a copy-edit, and finally the book will be proofread. Typically a freelance copy-editor will be assigned to your book once it has gone through the structural and line edit. The copy-editor's job is to make the language as tight as possible, to check for inconsistencies, and to point out small linguistic errors in the text. The book is also proofread.

In the meantime, as the books go through these stages, your publisher will be working hard behind the scenes to build an appetite and audience for your book. The editor will need to get everyone in the publishing company excited and enthused. Sometimes this is by sending out the manuscript, or giving away early copies internally. They need to show the strength of your writing and the commerciality of the book to everyone, in order to get everyone to believe in the potential of the book. There are many different strands within a publishing house, alongside the editor.

THE ART DEPARTMENT

The editor will draw up a brief to send to the art department for how they want the cover of your book to look. The editor will often involve the author and agent in this process, asking them if they have any ideas for how they want it to look. Several of my authors keep online scrapbooks of images that inspired them during the writing process: the editors have also looked at these and used them as inspiration when briefing the cover artwork.

Often, covers go through various iterations before they reach a point where everyone is happy with them. The cover needs to position the book for the audience: it needs to convey the subject of the book, its tone and the genre. It needs to be intriguing and convince the reader to pick the book up. For a young adult audience, it is important that the cover looks right for their age group. The art department will work hard to make sure that it speaks to their age range, by looking at albums, film posters and websites, and considering other books in a similar area that have performed well.

Sometimes an author is unhappy with the jacket, and an agent's role is to mediate between author and editor, to ensure that a front cover everyone is happy with is the one that goes on the front of the book. Often, however, the cover looks nothing like the one the author had imagined; but it precisely captures the spirit of the book in a very attractive way.

> ## Key idea
>
>
> When sending in a submission, many authors attach a home-drawn cover for their book. While this can be an interesting reference point for you, the likelihood is that the actual cover will look very different – publishers are practised at creating jackets that appeal to retailers and to the target market.

MARKETING

The marketing department is in charge of paid promotions to support your book. Before the Internet became mainstream, in the late 1990s, most marketing budgets were spent on print advertising: adverts on the underground or newspaper adverts, for example. Nowadays, a lot of marketing takes place online. Various promotions can advertise your books on Facebook, or Instagram, using algorithms to calculate who they should appear to, based on their browsing history and other interests. Very few books get major marketing campaigns to support their launches, since they are very expensive. However, the marketing team will always be looking for creative ways to make a book stand out to readers, such as through running partnerships with brands, or by exclusive competitions.

The marketing department will also be responsible for writing the blurb on the back of the book.

PUBLICITY

The publicist's job is to get the press to review a book, or to run features by the author. There is limited space in the traditional press to run reviews of YA novels so the publicist has to convince the reviewers, through a gripping press release and a great cover, that it is worth their time dedicating review space to the book. Publicists also target book bloggers, who write reviews of books on their blogs. Some blogs have very small readerships, but the biggest review blogs can get hundreds of thousands of hits and have a positive impact on sales of a book if they really get behind it.

Publicists will also pitch features, written by the author, to magazines, blogs and newspapers. For example, perhaps an author has written a YA novel about teen sexual assault, and they experienced that themselves as a teenager. If they were willing to write about it, then the publicist might pitch a feature about their real-life experience, to publish in a magazine.

Publicists will also pitch news stories about books, wherever possible. For example, *The Miniaturist* by Jessie Burton had news stories pitched about it once it had become the bestselling debut novel of the year. That meant that it had space in the press that was outside the reviews and features sections, which meant that more people heard of it and were likely to pick it up.

Publicists will also organize events and signings for authors. Sometimes this will just be the author doing a couple of signings at local bookshops, but sometimes the author will go on a book-signing tour of the country and end up signing thousands of copies for fans in each bookshop they visit.

SALES

The sales team's job is to pitch the book to retailers. They will present key titles to the retailers – for example to Amazon, Waterstones and WHSmith – and try to convince them to order solid quantities of the book and to put it into their promotions in shop or online. The marketing plans, the publicity plans, the cover and, of course, the book itself are all used to help convince the retailers what quantities of the book to take. If the author already has a sales track record, it can be helpful to promoting the book, but if they are a debut author, a lot comes down to the publication plans, the package and the manuscript itself. There is limited space in shops, so booksellers need to make sure that they are focusing on giving the space to the best books, which will hopefully sell very successfully for them.

The sales team negotiates the promotional packages, manages the orders, and negotiates the discounts they offer to the retailers. They are a key part of the process of selling a book with a traditional publisher.

The international sales team has to do a similar job to the sales team, but with bookshops around the British Commonwealth. Often, foreign bookstores will want the books in a different format from the home market, and they will push the books into different promotions that work for them. Sometimes the author might sign copies for retailers, or, on rare occasions, visit the bookshops abroad and do signings there.

There are, of course, other parts of publishing houses as well: digital account managers, special sales teams, communications managers and more! Publishing companies, especially big ones, are very practised at selling books and the big pro of signing with a traditional publisher – as well as receiving an advance – is that the weight of promoting and selling the book is taken from your shoulders, and put on to theirs.

> ## Key idea
>
>
> A lot of people make up the team inside a publishing house, working behind the scenes to produce and publish a novel.

Write

By this stage, you should have looked at the opening chapter of your novel so many times that you might well know it by heart. Have a go at rewriting it, from memory. Do not look at it again before doing the exercise, but try to recreate it as much as possible by heart. Perhaps it will be shorter than the original opening chapter, or use different descriptors, or bring in the main character earlier – but try to reproduce it as faithfully as you can from memory.

Edit

Look again at the cover letter you have written for your work. Analyse whether it is too long, or too brief. Does it tell the publisher enough about the author? Does it lay out the genre of the novel clearly and show an awareness of comparative titles? Is it intriguing? If not, redraft it, until you have created something very polished. Then compare this to the original cover letter you wrote to send out to agents. What did you learn from this exercise? How can you apply it to your own cover letter for agents?

Directly submitting to publishers

Most traditional publishers will only accept submissions via a literary agent, but some imprints do accept direct submissions, and it is worth considering these. Do your research into your ideal publisher, and check to see whether they are accepting direct submissions. It could be worth your while targeting them directly at the same time as submitting to agents. It is important to consider the small print. What rights are they requesting? Will the book be in physical or digital only? What will you be paid? Publishing is a business, and the deal you get from directly negotiating with a publisher is often very different from the deal you get when an experienced agent is the one to negotiate for you.

A lot of digital-only presses are a middle ground between more traditional publishing and self-publishing. They accept submissions directly from authors and they provide you with an editor, cover designer and publishing team. They also often offer a higher royalty than traditional houses offer. However, it is worth doing your research about them before signing any contract. Which other authors do they publish? How many authors do they have on their books? What can they offer you that you couldn't do yourself by self-publishing?

Key idea

If you have submitted directly to a publisher, be very careful whenever signing a contract: make sure that you are not signing away rights that you will regret in a few years, if the relationship breaks down. Make sure to be clear about what they are offering, and what they expect from you.

Den Patrick

'Remember, contracts are there for when things go wrong. It's important they serve both parties so you need someone who will negotiate on your behalf to serve your interests. A good agent will not only know the nuances of contract negotiation, but also provide a barrier between you and the nitty-gritty of the business conversation. Nothing kills creative energy more than worrying about contracts in my experience.'

Self-publishing

Self-publishing is a growing industry around the world. In the past, it was very hard to get your book published independently, but nowadays, with the advent of Amazon, it has become a lot easier for authors to get their books published online.

Some authors choose to be wholly self-published, even if they have approaches from traditional publishers. Some authors choose to be hybrid authors, which means that some of their books are published traditionally, and others are self-published. This can make sense, as some books may have a big commercial readership, whereas others might be more personal, or have more of a niche audience. This smaller audience might make it more difficult for a publisher to take the book on, but would not put off the fans who might still read it if it was self-published.

Self-publishing offers authors control over every aspect of the process, from the edits, to the cover, to the price promotions the book goes into online. Some authors relish this control, as it means they can communicate directly with their readership, and understand their market and which promotions work and which do not.

A great advantage of self-publishing is how easy and fast it is. Rather than having to send your book to agents and publishers and wait for months for them to respond, you can quickly and easily put your book online and start getting feedback right away. This can be a great boon to the author, but can also be a very real pitfall as it can encourage writers to not put the same care and attention into self-publishing as they would into trying to get traditionally published.

 ## Nick Spalding, self-published best-selling author

'Self-publishing has given lots of people the ability to write lots of books and get them out there. People need to remember that just because you can, doesn't mean you should.'

Another advantage of self-publishing is that you can get direct feedback from your readers. Sometimes a publisher might not be interested in a book as it would not perhaps sell enough copies to make it worth their while, but that doesn't mean to say that it still wouldn't find a loyal core readership if it were put online. Readers can tell you of errors you have made, or characters they love, or things they hope to see more of, and you can apply that to your own novels going forward.

Some self-published writers self-publish because it allows them to publish faster than traditional publishing allows for. Most writers have one book a year published, two at most, but with self-publishing you can publish as many books as you have written, as quickly as you like. Amanda Hocking, for example, published nine ebooks in 2010 and 2011. A traditional publisher could never have published them physically as quickly as she could by doing it herself. She quickly built up a market, and by March 2011 had sold more than 900,000 copies of her ebooks. Things started slowly for her, selling 45 copies in two weeks, but once she started sending her work to bloggers to review, and pricing the books low, she found that sales began to take off. However, it is worth noting that in 2011 she chose to sign a four-book deal with St Martin's Press, stating: 'I *only* want to be a writer,' Hocking said. 'I do not want to spend 40 hours a week handling emails, formatting covers, finding editors, etc. Right now, being me is a full-time corporation.'

As well as ceding control, in a major publishing deal, you also lose royalties. A typical UK publishing contract will pay 25 per cent of the net receipts for every ebook sold. With self-publishing, you are keeping, on average, 70 per cent of the net receipts for the book. With a traditional publishing contract, you also have to wait to receive your royalties. Once the advance has been earned out, royalties are calculated twice a year, so you might be waiting eight months to receive earlier royalties.

Snapshot

Look at the pros and cons of traditional and self-publishing. Make a list of three pros for each when it comes to your specific novel.

My advice to anyone considering self-publishing is that you should treat it as if you are running your own small business. You need to hire an editor and a proofreader, you need to get a cover professionally designed, and you need to have your own realistic marketing and publicity plan to put in action. A lot of writers self-publish at the same time as submitting to agents, but put little thought into their plan of action to make their ebooks stand out. Nowadays, hundreds of thousands of ebooks are uploaded to Amazon, and most of them are priced very cheaply. How are you going to make yours stand out?

Some YA writers sell most of their books through physical editions. Some former teachers, or people who are used to speaking to children and teenagers, make a living through visiting schools and selling their books at the end of their talks. Through using local press and contacts, and selling directly through their website, they can run a very successful business. This is not a small undertaking: it is important to consider your business plan, the cost of having your books printed, whether you will be able to visit schools and speak to the children, and whether you have contacts in local press that you can utilize. If you are confident in your ability to make a success through this route, it can be an exciting and rewarding endeavour.

If what you want is for family, friends, and other like-minded people to read your words, then self-publishing absolutely can be the right way to go. If you have a polished novel, with a professional package, and you want to retain control over the process, and have a clear idea of how to launch your book online, then absolutely go for self-publishing. There are numerous resources for self-publishers out there, and the Alliance of Independent Authors (ALLi) is a great help. It describes itself as: 'The professional association for authors who self-publish. This global, non-profit organization brings together the world's best indie authors, advisors and services, offering contacts and campaigns, education and collaboration – together with trusted guidance on how to self-publish well.'

 Focus point

If you do choose to self-publish, you should treat it professionally. Prepare a press release for your book, or hire someone to do so, and decide how to publicize and market your work. Do not rush into the process headlong but make sure to give it care and attention.

 James Oswald, self-published and traditionally published author

'Self-publishing, at least in ebook form, is very easy and very rapid, both in setting up a book to sell, and in getting feedback and sales figures… The ease of it is perhaps both its greatest advantage and its greatest weakness.'

Pros and cons

SELF-PUBLISHING PROS

- No barriers to entry
- Complete creative control
- Quick to do and quick to get feedback for
- Higher royalties than traditional publishing offers
- Closer relationship with your readership
- Receiving money within a month rather than waiting for royalty periods twice a year

SELF-PUBLISHING CONS

- Can be expensive upfront to have the book edited, formatted, and have a front cover designed
- Difficult to know how to make your book stand out in a crowded marketplace
- Most broadsheets will not review self-published books, although this is slowly changing
- Most mainstream prizes will not accept entries from self-published books
- You have to be responsible for every aspect of the process, not just the writing of the novel
- Difficult to have your book distributed in physical edition in bookshops

TRADITIONAL PUBLISHING PROS

- A team at a publisher including editor, publicist and marketer
- Greater distribution in physical editions than in self-publishing
- An advance being paid to you upfront
- A feeling of greater legitimacy
- Someone else taking care of the business side and freeing up your time to write

TRADITIONAL PUBLISHING CONS

- A very competitive market so difficult to find an agent, and to find a publishing deal
- Ceding control over the finished package to someone else who might have a different creative vision from you
- Having to wait to receive royalties
- Receiving smaller royalties per sold book than you would by self-publishing

There is no 'right' route into publishing – every book is different, and every author is different. Some authors will self-publish several novels before traditionally publishing one. Others will always self-publish their works because they prefer to retain the control. Some will always aim for traditional publishing and never attempt self-publishing as they are too busy. People on both sides will give you convincing arguments for their chosen way, but really, it comes down to what you want to achieve for your book, and how best you think you can achieve it.

Workshop

Look back at the first chapter of your book that you rewrote from memory. Compare it to your original first chapter. Ask yourself the following questions:

- Which is stronger and more interesting?
- Which feels more polished?
- What have you lost in the version you wrote from memory?
- What have you gained?
- Which version of the chapter will you keep, going forward?

The idea is, that from writing the first chapter again from memory, you actually keep only the important and interesting text. You lose the filler, keeping only the killer! What did you learn from this exercise, and did you apply it to the other chapters of your novel? I am not suggesting you rewrite all of it from memory, but it can be an interesting technique to make you analyse what is most important about a novel.

Congratulations on finishing the course! You have learned a lot during your reading of the book. You have learned how to come up with ideas, how to plan a novel, and build a world, and develop interesting characters. If you look back over the exercises you have completed over the course of the book, you should have found that your writing has improved with every exercise. Your writing career is a journey – perhaps a long journey – and everything you write will help you better understand what you need to do to become a better, and stronger, novelist. By finishing this book, and finishing your own book, you have shown persistence, strength of character and passion. These are all crucial traits in a novelist.

Whether you decide to put your novel away and start a new one, or you begin the journey into attempting publication, you should be pleased with everything you have achieved. Next time someone asks you what you enjoy doing, you can tell them 'I am a writer' – and you should feel very proud of that.

Online resources

Absolute Write

A great place to meet like-minded people and discuss every aspect of the writing process

http://www.absolutewrite.com/forums/

Alliance of Independent Authors

This is an organization for authors who self-publish. The website is full of news, advice and ways to contact like-minded people if this is the path you wish to investigate.

http://allianceindependentauthors.org

Archive of Our Own

This is a fan-created non-profit archive of fanfiction. Some writers cut their teeth here, and it can be an interesting site to upload your own work, or read other pieces of fanfiction.

http://archiveofourown.org

NaNoWriMo

The official website of the popular annual novel-writing event. You can sign up here, track your progress and meet other writers.

http://nanowrimo.org

SCBWI

The Society of Children's Book Writers and Illustrators is a fantastic resource with events, support and resources.

http://www.scbwi.org

Wattpad

Wattpad is an archive of free stories. You can share your own, or read others'.

https://www.wattpad.com/signup

Index